S0-CBX-783

JOHN

JOHN
A new look at the 4th gospel
*
Norman R. Ericson & Lloyd M. Perry

Tyndale House
Publishers, Inc.
Wheaton, Illinois

L. I. F. E Bible College
LIBRARY
1100 COVINA BLVD
SAN DIMAS, CA 91773

Scripture quotations are from the New American Standard Bible
© 1960, 1962, 1963, 1968, 1971
by The Lockman Foundation, La Habra, California.

First printing, October 1981

Library of Congress Catalog Card Number 81-50542
ISBN 0-8423-1892-5 paper
Copyright © 1981 by Norman R. Ericson and Lloyd M. Perry
All rights reserved
Printed in the United States of America

226.506
E45j

L. I F. E Bible College
LIBRARY
1100 COVINA BLVD
SAN DIMAS, CA 91773

CONTENTS

A study of the Greek text clarifies the meaning of words
and phrases in the English Versions. Each thematic
segment is analyzed by using six interrogatives. Content
comments are included from historical, geographical,
and textual material.

042024

The best comes last. The fourth Gospel is the Gospel of Gospels, the holy of holies in the New Testament. . . . The Gospel according to John is the most original, the most important, the most influential book in all literature. . . . It is simple as a child and sublime as a seraph, gentle as a lamb and bold as an eagle, deep as the sea and high as the heavens.

PHILIP SCHAFF, *History of the Christian Church* vol. 1, pages 675, 688.

042024

INTRODUCTION

It is important to know what the Bible says. The preacher cannot preach the Word without knowing the Word. The leader of a Bible class cannot lead the students into the Scriptures until the teacher has first explored the treasures. The believer cannot live in accordance with the Word unless he realizes the limits of the Word. The searcher for truth will be blessed as he explores God's mine of treasure, the Bible.

This book has been prepared as an aid for preacher, teacher, believer, and searcher. The authors of this volume believe that there is blessing in believing the testimony of John relating to the Lord Jesus Christ.

This fourth Gospel may be the best known book of the sixty-six included in God's library, the Bible. Spiritual experience and the Christlike life receive the stamp of importance. The combination of childlike simplicity and contemplative profundity highlight the central thought of the Gospel of John, the incarnation, the Word became flesh.

This book, dealing with the inductive Bible study of the Gospel of John, consists of four main sections. The first section outlines and provides examples of ten Bible study methods as these relate to the Gospel of John. The second section surveys and analyzes the thematic segments of the Gospel. A thematic segment is a unit designed to develop one main thought. The segments bear a special relationship to the paragraphing. This approach to the content provides a long-range or telescopic view. The third section surveys the more minute features of the content. The English translation is compared with the Greek text. This provides a microscopic view of the content since it analyzes words and phrases. Once the content of the Gospel has been surveyed and analyzed, it should be shared. The fourth section provides suggestions for personal devotional study and the preparation of material for sharing with others.

The Gospel of John offers a unique perspective on the life of Christ. In meaningful ways it is unlike the portrayal in Matthew, Mark, and Luke. An awareness of these differences enhances one's appreciation of both Gospel traditions. The three Synoptic Gospels are so much alike as to be nearly identical in such features as length of ministry, nature and order of events, content of Jesus' teaching, and literary style.

In the Synoptic Gospels the ministry of Jesus appears to last but one year since it moves in a single sweep from baptism to resurrection, from Galilee to Jerusalem. John, however, reports repeated trips to Jerusalem and specifies at least three Passovers. Thus the public ministry in John is at least two years long, or even three if the feast in John 5:1 is a Passover.

Similarly the basic literary unit is different in the two traditions. In the Synoptic Gospels the individual paragraph is the organizing unit. The deeds of Jesus are reported simply, containing question and answer, or miracle and public response. Jesus' teachings are either climactic statements at the end of a paragraph or collections of paragraphs as in the Sermon on the Mount, the commission to the disciples, or the apocalyptic discourse. And the content of Jesus' teaching centers around the arrival of the Kingdom of God with the demand for living according to the intentions of God. Jesus rarely speaks about Himself, and even then speaks in the third person by the use of the cryptic title "Son of Man."

In contrast, the basic structure of the Gospel of John is deed followed by interpretative discourse. This results in extensive dialogue (the Samaritan woman), complicated plots (the man born blind), and complex discourses which extend for several paragraphs. Only in John do the people in Jesus' ministry take on personality, express real feelings, and interrogate Jesus. The reader begins to "know" Nicodemus, the Samaritan woman, the lame man, and even the family of the blind man, along with Mary and Martha. And it is John alone who reports such marvelous discourses as those on the birth from above, the "Comforter," and Jesus' intercessory prayer.

Most striking is the way Jesus spoke of Himself in the Gospel of John. He clearly announced His special relationship to the Father, a oneness with God which led the Jews to charge Him with blasphemy. He was aware of His preexistence; knew that He spoke the words and performed the deeds of His father. This self-understanding was climaxed in the "I am" statements. These occur both with predicate ("bread," "light," "door," "shepherd," "resurrection," "way," and "vine") and more importantly without: "If you do not believe that I am you will die in your sins." Even His death is declared to be the mode of His glorification as He was lifted up by means of the cross to where He was before, enjoying the glory of His Father. The prologue of John captures these thoughts magnificently by the announcement that the preexistent divine Word became flesh—the eternal Word and created flesh became one!

Another major difference in the two traditions relates to contents and order. The Synoptic Gospels include the same basic events and report them generally in the same order. All three report the Lord's baptism, the temptation, parables, transfiguration, and the last supper. Yet these very events are either not mentioned at all in John, or are merely alluded to as if already familiar to the readers. Except for the last week in Jerusalem, John shares only two paragraphs with the Synoptic Gospels: the feeding of the five thousand and the walking on the water. But he reports five additional signs: water turned to wine, restoration of the nobleman's son, the healing of the lame man, healing of the blind man, and the raising of Lazarus. A striking difference is also seen in two other events. The cleansing of the temple in John occurs on Jesus' first visit to Jerusalem, but it is a part of Passion Week in the Synoptics. And the Holy Spirit is breathed upon the disciples by the resurrected Christ even prior to his ascension!

Finally, the literary methods of John are distinct from the straight narrative and didactic style of the Synoptics. John made use of Hebrew poetry (statements with parallel thoughts), inserted editorial comments (7:39), and highlighted misunderstanding by the audience ("Destroy this temple"). He emphasized double meaning (born again/born from above), irony ("Are you greater than our father Jacob?"), contradiction ("I do not go up to the feast" . . . "Then He . . . went up . . .") and repetition of words for emphasis (believe, father, light, truth). And through all of his narrative we sense the vividness of the present tense ("There *is* . . .) and eyewitness detail (". . . a pool with five porticoes").

This vividness of action and the descriptive detail suggest an early date for the Gospel. The impression is heightened by the absence of any allusion to the destruction of Jerusalem and the emphasis upon the "beloved disciple." It has been suggested therefore that this Gospel was written as early as the sixties—soon after the events and before the destruction of Jerusalem. More commonly, however, it is thought to have been written in the nineties. Evidence for this includes the presumed familiarity of the readers with the basic Gospel events, the awareness of a second generation of Christians (17:20), the ignorance of the readers regarding the city of Jerusalem and her political-religious tensions, and the suggestions of patristic writers that this is the latest of the Gospels.

Since the canonical Gospels do not name either the author or the recipients (but notice Luke 1:3), this information must be determined from internal evidence and from early church tradition. The statement of purpose in John 20:30, 31 ("that you may believe") does not specify whether the readers should "come to believe" (as non-Christians) or "grow in belief" (as new converts) or "remain firm in belief" (as Christians for some time).

Four times the Gospel mentions "the disciple whom Jesus loved" (13:23; 19:26; 21:7; and 21:20). Assuming that he was one of the inner three (Mark 9:2), only John the son of Zebedee qualifies as beloved disciple. James was executed in A.D. 44, and Peter is by name distinguished from the beloved disciple in 13:23, 24.

This internal evidence corresponds well with the statement of Irenaeus that the Apostle John wrote this Gospel at Ephesus. Irenaeus learned this from Polycarp, who was a disciple of the Apostle John. This combination of the Apostle John and the city of Ephesus explains both the vivid eyewitness quality of the Gospel as well as the impression of an audience distant in time and geography.

The nature of Ephesus and the features of the Gospel also correspond. Ephesus was a strong Christian center since the early fifties and was thus familiar with the basic Gospel events. The strong Jewish interest in the Gospel corresponds to the significant Jewish population in Ephesus. The Gospel's dimunition of the Baptist reminds us of Acts 18:25—19:3. The emphasis upon the real incarnation gives meaningful contrast to the Hellenistic separation of (good) spirit from (evil) matter. And the centrality of Ephesus among the Asian churches gives a strategic setting for such an important gospel message in a larger Greek environment, to persons in various stages of belief. Thus the Gospel of God's love for the world was written in a cosmopolitan center, for a circle of churches maturing in the faith, with a clear and effective message for each kind of person. And from one who had lived with Jesus Christ!

John excels in the depths of divine mysteries. Its combination of minute historical detail with lofty spiritual teaching, its testimony to the person and work of the Lord Jesus, and the preparation it makes for the foundations of Christian doctrine make it appear as deep as the deepest sea and as lofty as a mighty mountain.

Little interest is shown in forms and ceremonies. Institutional religion held little interest for the author of this Gospel. John meditated upon that which he saw and heard and, being inbreathed by the Holy Spirit, he put down his conclusions regarding them. Here is a commentary as well as a biography. This Gospel is an interpretation of Christ rather than an orderly presentation of His life.

This Gospel should be read with joy and reverence. It seems as though a cloud of glory hovers over each page and heaven seems to surround us as we read.

The simplicity of language is evident in the Greek text as well as in the English translations. New converts find that it is profitable to begin their reading and study of the Word of God with this Gospel. After years of digging in this mine of treasure, these same converts will still find that there is more treasure beyond.

This Gospel is the consummation of the Gospels as the Gospels are of all the Scriptures.

ORIGEN

John excels in the depths of divine mysteries.

JEROME

It is the unique, tender, genuine, chief Gospel, far preferable to the other three. . . . Should a tyrant succeed in destroying the Holy Scriptures and only a single copy of the Epistle to the Romans and the Gospel according to John escape him, Christianity would be saved.

LUTHER from D. A. Hayes *John and His Writings* (New York: Methodist Book Concern, 1917), p. 77.

One

DISCOVERING CONTENT THROUGH INDUCTIVE METHODS OF BIBLE STUDY

In this chapter ten methods of Bible study will be applied to the Gospel of John. After studying John in these ways it will be possible to use the same methods on other books of the Bible.

THE BOOK STUDY METHOD

Themes or titles for the book
The Witness of John to the Deity of Jesus
The Gospel of Believing
Jesus Christ, the Son of God
The Book of Signs and of Glory
The Gospel of Faith
The Book of the Great "I Am"
The Gospel of the Love of God

Who was the human author?
John, the Apostle, "the disciple whom Jesus loved (John 13:23; 19:26; 20:2, 8; and 21:7, 20).

He was also the author of 1, 2 and 3 John and of the Revelation. Only Paul wrote more books in the New Testament than John.

John is not named in this Gospel, but is mentioned thirty-five times in the other Gospels, and three times in the books of Acts (3:1; 4:13; 8:14.) Paul called him a "pillar" of the Jerusalem Church (Gal. 2:9).

His hometown was Bethsaida in Galilee, not far from Capernaum (John 1:44; Luke 5:10).

He was a cousin of Jesus. His mother was Salome, sister of Mary (Mark 16:1; Matt. 27:56; John 19:25). Salome was among the women who provided for Jesus out of their own means (Luke 8:3; Mark 15:40) and was present at the crucifixion.

He was first a follower of John the Baptist (John 1:35) and was present at the baptism of Jesus (Acts 1:22).

He was one of the first disciples called to follow Jesus (John 1:35-40; Mark 1:16-20).

He and his brother James were high-spirited Galileans (Mark 10:37), known as "Sons of Thunder" (Mark 3:17; Luke 9:49, 50). John was capable of fiery zeal (1 John 2:22; 3:8, 15; 4:20).

There were at least three stages in his fellowship with Christ: Attachment (John 1:40), Discipleship (Matt. 4:21, 22), and Apostleship (Luke 6:13, 14).

He was part of the inner circle with Peter and James (Mark 5:37; 9:2; 14:33).

Jesus directed John and Peter to prepare the final Passover (Luke 22:8) and Jesus committed the care of His mother to John at the crucifixion (John 19:25-27).

John lived to a great age (21:23), and was the only one of the twelve Apostles not martyred.

John was an eyewitness of the things he described (John 1:14; 19:35; 21:24; 1 John 1:1, 3).

As a writer his dominant characteristic is contemplative receptivity.

When was the book written?

The probable date is about A.D. 90, when there was need for advanced teaching concerning the nature of faith. Some have suggested that it was written before the destruction of Jerusalem in A.D. 70. There is a vividness in this Gospel appropriate to an early date.

Where was the book written?

The Gospel of John was written in Ephesus, in the Roman province of Asia. This is where John lived and died, according to Irenaeus, Jerome, and many others.

To whom was the book written?

Matthew was written to the Jews of Syria and Palestine; Mark was written to the gentiles of Rome; and Luke was written for all gentiles. John, however, was written in a Jewish perspective with a concern for the whole world (John 7:35; 10:16; 11:52).

What purposes was the book designed to serve?
There was an evangelistic purpose: That the readers might believe and have life through the name of Jesus Christ (20: 30, 31).
There were several doctrinal purposes:
To insist on the incarnation of the Christ
To emphasize that Jesus came from God.
To assure that Jesus was greater than John the Baptist
To clarify the presence of Jesus Christ through His Spirit
There was a literary purpose: To supplement their knowledge of the gospel: Six of the thirty-five miracles recorded by the four Gospels are peculiar to John:
Water to wine, 2:1-11
The nobleman's son, 4:46-54
The man at the pool, 5:1-9
The man born blind, 9:1-7
The raising of Lazarus, 11:17-44
The catch of fish, 21:1-14
There was a historical purpose: To explain how Jesus came to be crucified, and give evidence for his resurrection.
There was a religious purpose: To give an understanding of the ordinances from the life of Jesus.
There was a cosmological purpose: To show that Jesus is the Savior of the entire world.

What peculiar or repeated words occur within the book?
know 141 (*ginosko* 56 and *oida* 85)
Father 137 (of God 120)
believe 98
the Jews 68
world 78
glory 20
truth 25
true 23
name 25
Spirit 15 (Holy Spirit 3)
Comforter 4
Word (logos) 40 (The Word 4)
Abide 40

see (five different words) 114
love 56
verily 50
witness 47
abide 40
send 32
life 36 (Eternal Life 17)
live 17
I am 31 (by Jesus 28)
light 24
born 18 (born again 2)
work 35
sign 17
feast 17
judge 19

The word "that" (Gr. *hina*) occurs 145 times. It emphasizes the divine purpose (John 1:7; 3:15; 5:23; 9:3; 11:4; 17:12; 20:31).

The word "therefore" (Gr. *oun*) occurs 190 times. It emphasizes cause and relationship (John 2:22; 3:29; 4:53; 5:18; 8:36; 11:54; 18:4; 21:7).

The Gospel of John has 112 words which are peculiar to it, such as the following:

head waiter
barley (loaves)
spittle
expelled-from-synagogue
stench (stink)
dwelling-place
The Pavement (mosaic)
worshiper
Feast of Tabernacles
(swimming) pool
Feast of Dedication
money-box
branch
breathe upon

The Gospel of Luke has 261 unique words, Matthew has 112, and Mark has 79. John has the smallest vocabulary of the four Gospels with 1,011 words, but uses his words most profoundly. Luke uses 2,055 different words, Matthew uses 1,690, and Mark uses 1,270.

How would you characterize the style?

The style of this Gospel is simple, but the message is profound. The simplicity of sentences and vocabulary becomes majestic by the solemn directness.

There is reflective contemplation (3:16-21) and dramatic dialogue (8:21-30).

There is frequent repetition of words (1:1; 1:10; 5:31-34; 10:11, 14).

Word variation is also extensive: three words for "go away" in 16:5-10; three words for grieve in 16:20-22; two words for "ear" in 18:10; and two words for "love" in 21:15-17.

Phrases are often repeated, either exactly (8:21; 8:22; 13:33) or with slight variation (12:31; 14:30; 16:11; and 14:26; 15:26; 16:7).

John includes ironic statements (4:12; 7:42; 11:50) words with double meaning (3:3 again/above; 3:8 wind/spirit; 12:32, 33 exalt/crucify); and misunderstanding by Jesus' hearers (3:4; 4:11).

Many sentences appear in the parallelism of Hebrew poetry; synonymous (6:35; 6:55; 7:34) and antithetic (8:35; 3:20, 21).

There are no parables in the Gospel of John. The word used in 10:6; 16:25; and 16:29 is not the same word as used in the Synoptics. The word used by John emphasizes the figure of speech, or the "darkness" of a saying. It might be called a "wayside discourse."

John emphasizes the symbolism of Jewish festivals and Old Testament types which are realized in Jesus (1:29; 3:14; 6:31-33).

There are thirteen quotations of the Old Testament taken from the Septuagint, not immediately from the Hebrew.

Even with the emphasis on the historical setting, this is clearly the spiritual Gospel (3:5; 4:24; 6:63; 14:17; 20:22).

The work and message of the Father are presented in the deeds and words of the Son.

The Gospel is composed of deed and discourse. Each miracle of Jesus is explained by His own discourse which follows.

This is the Gospel of conflict: between light and darkness, between belief and unbelief, between Jesus and "the Jews."

What does the book teach about the Godhead?

God, the Father: 120 references.

Holy Spirit: sixteen references

Christ as the "I am": sixteen references

Christ as the "logos": four references

THE SYNTHETIC METHOD

Synthesis is the process of putting the contents together. *Syn* means "together" and *thesis* means "to put." After repeated readings of the material, the student should then attempt to organize the material into outline form.

Outline 1 of John's Gospel
1:1-18 Prologue
   1:1-4
   1:5-11
   1:12-18
1:19-12:50 The Public Manifestation of Christ to the World
   1:19—4:54 Consideration
      1:19-51
      2:1-11
      2:12-22
      2:23—3:21
      3:22-36
      4:1-42
      4:43-54
   5:1—10:42 Conflict
      5:1-18
      5:19-47
      6:1-21
      6:22-71
      7:1-13
      7:14-36
      7:37-52
      7:53—8:11
      8:12-30
      8:31-59
      9:1-41
      10:1-21
      10:22-42
   11:1—12:50 Cleavage
      11:1-53
      11:54—12:11
      12:12-50
13:1-17-26 The Private Manifestation of Christ to the
         Disciples
   13:1—15:27 Warning of His Departure
      13:1-30

13:31—14:31
15:1-27
16:1-33 Promise of the Coming of the Holy Spirit
16:1-6
16:7-15
16:16-33
17:1-26 Prayer for His Disciples
18:1—20:31 The Perfect Manifestation of Christ in His Passion
18:1—19:16 Prosecution
19:17-42 Crucifixion
20:1-31 Resurrection
21:1-25 Epilogue

Outline 2 of John's Gospel (Signs and "I Am's")
1:1-18 Prologue

1:19—4:54 Time of Consideration and Contacts
Sign 1: 2:1-12 Turned water to wine
                    Power over nature

Sign 2: 4:46-54 Healed nobleman's son
                    Power over disease

5:1—6:71 Time of Controversy
Sign 3: 5:1-18 Impotent man healed
                    Power over time

Sign 4: 6:1-14 Feeding of five thousand
                    Power over matter

Sign 5: 6:15-21 Walked on water
                    Power over forces of nature

"I am the bread of life" (6:35).

7:1—11:53 Time of Conflict
Sign 6: 9:1-41 Healed the blind man
                    Power over physical problems

Sign 7: 11:1-44 Raised Lazarus
                    Power over physical problems

"I am the light of the world" (8:12).
"I am the door of the sheep" (10:7).
"I am the good shepherd" (10:11).
"I am the resurrection and the life" (11:25).

11:54—12:36a Time of Crisis

12:36b—17:26 Time of Conference
  "I am the way, and the truth, and the life" (14:6).
  "I am the true vine" (15:1).

18:1—20:31 Time of Consummation

21:1-25 Epilogue
  NOTE: The "I am" verses and the signs.

THE HISTORICAL METHOD

Thematic	Chronological	Geographical
1:1-18 Prologue		
1:19—4:54 Consideration	1:19—4:54 A.D. 27	1:19-42 Judea
Nicodemus		1:43—2:12 Galilee
Samaritan woman	2:23—3:21 Passover	2:13—3:36 Jerusalem
Nobleman	2:12, 13 Passover	4:1-45 Samaria
John		4:45, 46 Galilee
5:1—6:71 Controversy		
Impotent Man	4:46—5:47 A.D. 28	4:46—5:47 Jerusalem
Unity with the Father	5:1 Feast of Purim	5:1-47 Judea
5,000 fed	6:1—10:42 A.D. 29	
Walking on the sea	6:4 Passover at hand	6:1-7:9 Galilee
	6:1-15 A.D. 29	
7:1—11:54 Conflict		7:10—10:40 Jerusalem
Jews seek Him	7:2 Feast of Taber-nacles	8:10—10:21 Judea
Woman in adultery	10:2 Feast of Dedi-cation	10:22-39 Judea
Light of the world	11:54-57 Passover	10:40—11:17 Perea
Sent from the Father	11:1-54 A.D. 30	
Good shepherd		
Raising of Lazarus		

11:54—20:31
Culmination

With friends	12:1 Passover	12:1 Jerusalem
Triumphal entry	13:1 Before Passover	11:17—20:31 Judea
Summary of claims		
Second coming		
True vine		
Encouragement and prayer		
Passion and resurrection		

Last Few Minutes

21:1-25 Epilogue	21 Galilee

NOTE:
Christ's ministry lasted for three years and five months

NOTE:
Jerusalem is in Judea about 30 miles from the Mediterranean and 18 miles from the Jordan

CHAPTER BIBLE STUDY/ John 14

1. *What is the theme of the chapter?*
   Faith in Christ and in His two comings
2. *Which is one of the best verses in the chapter?*
   Verse 14
3. *What personages are mentioned?*
   Philip, Judas, God the Father, Jesus, Spirit of Truth, Thomas
4. *What are the commands which we should obey?*
   Believe in the Father and likewise in Jesus, *Believe* that the Son is in the Father, and the Father is in the Son.
   Keep my [Christ's] commandments [Word].
   Do not be troubled.
5. *What are the promises which we should claim?*
   "*I go* to prepare a place for you" (v. 2).
   "*I will come again,* and receive you to Myself; that where I am, there you may be also " (v. 3).
   ". . . ask in My name, that will I do" (v. 13).
   "I will not leave you as orphans; *I will come* to you" (v. 18).

"I will ask the Father, and He will give you another
Helper, that He may be with you forever; that is the Spirit
of truth" (vv. 16, 17).
"I leave my peace with you" (v. 27).

6. *What are the lessons which we should remember?*
That Christ is the cure for our spiritual heart failure
(vv. 1, 27).
Jesus is the way, the truth, and the life;
No one comes to the Father, but through Him (v. 6).
The works that we do shall be greater if we believe in
Christ (v. 12).
Asking in Christ's name is essential (vv. 14, 15) and by that
act on our part He will do it.
If we love Christ we will keep His commandments (v. 21).

7. *Which words and phrases did you like best?*
"Let not your heart be troubled" (vv. 1, 27).
"I will come again" (v. 3).
"If you ask me anything in My name I will do it" (v. 14).
"If you love Me you will keep my commandments"
(v. 15).
"Spirit of Truth . . . you know Him because he abides
with you and will be in you" (v. 17).
"Peace I leave with you; My peace I give to you; not as
the world gives, do I give to you" (v. 27).

8. *Which words kept recurring throughout the chapter?*
Father
believe
(pronouns such as Me, My)
abiding places, abide
know
see
love

9. *Which words were not clear as to their meaning?*
"abides"—not a familiar word
"comforter"—special meaning
"commandments"—not specified here

10. *What logical reasons can you detect for the inclusion of this
chapter in the Bible?*
Because Jesus had announced His departure through
crucifixion the disciples needed assurance. Jesus declared
that He would send a replacement (The Comforter), and
that they would do greater works. He promised them the
answer to their prayers and His abiding peace. These are

the assurances of believers who wait for Him to come
for us.
11. *What are the errors of living which we should avoid?*
    Lack of faith
    Fear
12. *What does this chapter teach about God?*
    He can only be approached through Christ (v. 6).
    God loves those who love Christ and keep His Word
    (v. 21).

THE ANALYTICAL METHOD/ John 1:19-51

1. Who—
   a. John the Baptist—Described in the Prologue (1:6-8,
      31-34).
   b. Jews (Men of Judah)—Citizens of the Kingdom of
      Judah after the separation from the ten tribes. The name
      Jew in John's writings is used of those who were
      antagonistic toward Jesus. They were the blind followers
      of the Pharisees.
   c. Levites—The descendants of Levi, usually referring to
      those of the tribe who were not priests.
   d. Christ—Described in the Prologue section.
   e. Elias—The Greek form for Elijah (My God is Jehovah).
      A Tishbite of the inhabitants of Gilead. The grandest and
      most romantic character that Israel ever produced.
   f. Esaias—The Greek form for Isaiah. A prophet, the son of
      Amoz. The Hebrew name signifies "Jehovah is
      salvation." He prophesied concerning Judah and
      Jerusalem in the days of Uzziah, Jotham, Ahaz, and
      Hezekiah. He was the greatest of the writing prophets.
      He was a prophet-preacher, a man of genius in literary
      work, and a man of eloquence and wisdom.
   g. Pharisees (Separated Ones)—A religious party or
      school among the Jews at the time of Christ. They were
      largely middle-class laymen. Their origins go back to
      the Maccabean wars in a protest against the great
      Hellenistic influences. They stood for a strict
      observance of the Law. Their strictness led them to
      formulate a great variety of oral regulations adapted to
      new situations.
   h. Israel—The national name of the twelve tribes. It

lasted 321 years, from 1043-722 B.C. It is used here with a good connotation.

i. Holy Ghost—The third member of the Godhead.

j. Andrew—One of our Lord's Apostles and brother of Simon Peter. He was of Bethsaida, was formerly a disciple of John the Baptist and then left him to follow Jesus. He was placed fourth in importance among the disciples. It was said of him that he was crucified at Patrae in Achaia. He was quiet, approachable, friendly.

k. Simon Peter—The son of Jonas. He was a fisherman, born in Bethsaida. He was executed by crucifixion. One of Jesus' most intimate disciples. He was weak natured, but Christ was going to make him strong.

l. Philip—Born in Bethsaida. He was one of the earliest disciples to follow the Lord. He was among the group of disciples at Jerusalem after the ascension and on the day of Pentecost. He was stubborn.

m. Nathanael (God has given)—He was a disciple of Jesus and was born at Cana of Galilee. It was Philip who first brought Nathanael to Christ. He was skeptical.

2. What—John the Baptist made known to his inquirers that he was not the Christ, but was rather the forerunner of Christ. He witnessed to the fact that Jesus was the Lamb of God who takes away the sin of the world. Andrew, Philip, Peter, and Nathanael are directed to be disciples of Christ.

3. When—In A.D. 26, fall of 26 or spring of 27. It was the first year of Christ's ministry.

4. Where—Jerusalem (The city of peace) (1:19)—The supreme city in the world as to its influence upon the hopes and destiny of the world. It is thirty-two miles from the sea, eighteen from Jordan, twenty from Hebron, and thirty-six from Samaria. It is situated on the top of a ridge of hills. It had almost no commerce or business. It was the scene of the life, passion, cross, and grave of Christ. The city has had many earthquakes and has also undergone nearly twenty severe sieges.

Bathabara (Bethany—possibly Bethbarah) (1:28)—This is the place where John baptized Jesus. It was an obscure village near Bethabara and was fourteen miles below the Sea of Galilee.

Bethsaida (House of fish) (1:44)—It was in the land of Gennesaret. It was the place where the five thousand were fed. There was a Bethsaida of Galilee and one of Julias separated only by a small stream.

Nazareth (Offshoot) (1:45)—It was the ordinary residence of our Savior. It is situated among the hills which constitute the south ridges of Lebanon, just before the plain of Esdraelon. It was a city of fifteen to twenty thousand people. It is within the limits of the province of Galilee.

5. Why—This passage emphasizes that John knew he was only the forerunner of Jesus. It also gives the first reason for believing in Him because he was the Lamb of God who takes away the sins of the world. It thus introduces us to the main theme of the deity of Christ by giving the first basis for the thesis.

6. Wherefore—
   a. John was the forerunner of Christ.
   b. Jesus gained four disciples.
   c. Jesus' mission was set forth: He was to take away the sins of the world.

THE BIOGRAPHICAL METHOD

There are thirty-four individuals referred to in the Gospel of John. Twenty-three of these individuals are named and eleven are unnamed. Fifteen of the named individuals would appear to be rather special while eight are of secondary importance. It is helpful not only to put the individuals into categories of importance but also to give attention to the meaning of names since a name in Bible times had far more significance than it does at present.

John (Jehovah is merciful)—Mystic
Peter (A rock)—Impulsive
Andrew (Mighty one)—Missionary
Philip (Fond of horses)—Inquirer
Thomas (A "twin" in Aramaic; Didymus is the Greek form)—Cautious
Nathaniel (God has given) also known as Bartholomew—Guileless
James of Zebedee (from Jacob=supplanter)—Zealot
Judas, also known as Labbaeus (from Judah =praise)—Obscure
Judas Iscariot (Judah-Jehovah leads)—Traitor
John the Baptist (Jehovah is favored)—Austere
Nicodemus (Conqueror of the people)—Seeker
Pilate (Armed with a javelin)—Worldly
Martha (Lady)—Anxious

Mary (Beloved)—Worshiper
Mary Magdalene (Corpulent watchtower)—Devoted
Another method of studying biographically is to select a portion of the book in which several characters are referred to and list these together with what is said about them. In the Gospel of John, chapters 18 and 19 have several characters.

1. *Jesus*
   18:4-11 He gave Himself up
   18:6 Had resplendent glory
   18:20-23 Stated His ministry
   18:34—19:9-11 Spoke boldly before Pilate
   19:26, 27 Cared for His mother
   19:28-30 Simple yet profound in speech and action
2. *Judas*
   Betrayer—worldly—easily swayed by Satan
3. *Peter*
   18:10 Loyal, impulsive, fearful
   18:18, 25, 27 Denied his Lord
4. *Soldiers*
   18:3 They simply obeyed orders
   18:6, 12, 33 Overcome by Jesus majesty
   18:22 One struck Him—showing disrespect
   19:2, 3 They all mocked Him
   19:23, 24 They crucified Him, and divided His garments
   19:32, 33 They broke the legs of the other two
5. *Officers of the Chief Priests*
   18:3 They were the tools of their superiors
   18:10 Malchus was wounded by Peter
   19:6 Spiritually blind
6. *Annas* (Father-in-law of Caiaphas)
   Overbearing
7. *Caiaphas* (High Priest)
   18:14-19 Counselor to the Jews
   18:24-28 Inferior to Pilate
8. *John* ("another disciple")
   Influential—closest to Jesus
9. *The maid*
   Fearless
10. *Pilate*
    18:29-31 A shirker
    18:33-40 Insolent, haughty, cruel
    19:1-10 Overbearing, cruel
    19:4, 8, 12 Convinced of Jesus' innocence
    19:22 Cared for his job more than the truth.

11. *Joseph of Arimathea and Nicodemus*
    Disciples of Christ, tender, wealthy, discreet
12. *Others*
    The Father, Barabbas, Caesar, Two thieves, Jesus' mother, Jesus' aunt, Mary Magdalene
13. *Jews*
    Oppressive, adamant, cried "crucify Him"

Jesus had fourteen interviews in John's Gospel with one person and twenty interviews with groups of individuals. The following were among the most important.

1:47-51 Nathanael (Foreknowledge)
3:1-21 Nicodemus (New birth)
4:7-38 Woman of Samaria (Savior of the world)
4:48-50 Nobleman (The word of healing)
6:26-65 His followers (Bread from heaven)
8:3-11 Scribes and Pharisees (Personal sin)
8:19-59 Ones in the temple (Your father)
9:35-39 Blind man (Spiritual sight)
10:1-38 Jews (The sanctified one)
11:20-40 Mary and Martha (Life now)
12:23-36 His followers (Glorifications)
13:6-10 Simon Peter (Share with me)
13:21-38 Disciples (Troubled in spirit)
14:16-26 Disciples (The Spirit of truth)
18:33—19:11 Pilate (King of the Jews)
21:15-22 Simon Peter (Greater love)

1:38; 1:42; 2:4; 2:7, 8; 2:16-19; 5:18-47; 7:6-8; 7:16-34; 7:37, 38; 9:2-5; 11:4-15; 12:7, 8; 16:19-33; 18:4-8; 18:19-23; 20:15-17; 20:19-29; 21:5-12

A study can be made of special events connected with the experience of individuals. Here is a listing of the manner in which the disciples met death, according to early Christian tradition.

Matthew suffered martyrdom by the sword in Ethiopia.

Mark died at Alexandria, after being dragged through the streets of that city.

Luke was hanged on an olive tree in Greece.

John was put into a caldron of boiling oil but escaped death and was banished to Patmos.

Peter was crucified at Rome with his head downward.

James was beheaded at Jerusalem.

James the Less was thrown from a pinnacle of the temple and beaten to death below.

Philip was hanged against a pillar in Phrygia.
Bartholomew was flayed alive.
Andrew was bound to a cross, whence he preached to his persecutors until he died.
Thomas was run through the body at Coromandel, India.
Jude was shot to death with arrows.
Matthias was first stoned and then beheaded.
Barnabas was stoned to death by Jews at Salonica.
Paul was beheaded by Nero at Rome.

There is a method for studying an individual Bible character. This is set forth in the work by Culver and Perry entitled *How to Search the Scripture* (Grand Rapids: Baker, 1967). It involves answering a series of questions. The method can be illustrated by using Peter, one of the important characters in the Gospel of John.

1. What is the meaning of the individual's name?
    Peter—"rock" or "stone"; Simon—"hearing."
2. What is the ancestral background?
    Peter—Son of John; brother of Andrew; from Bethsaida, "Fish-town" (John 1).
3. What significant religious and secular crises occurred in this life?
    Peter—Religious crises: His call to follow Jesus; testing of a faith that failed; confessed Christ as Messiah; denied Christ three times; disagreement with the Lord about ceremony rites; rebuked by Paul before Galatian church; restored to fellowship with Jesus.
    —Secular crises: "Leaving all: (commercial life); in prison
4. What advantages for personal development were enjoyed?
    Peter—Follower of Jesus; one of the twelve; one of the inner circle.
5. What traits of character were manifested?
    Peter—Impulsive, energetic, courageous, inconsistent, and believing.
6. What important friendships did this person have?
    Peter—Apostle John, John Mark, Silvanus, Paul, Christ.
7. What important influences did this individual exert?
    Peter—A spokesman for the early disciples; leader of

the early church; first great preacher of the Christian Church; first Jewish Christian to have converts from among the Gentiles; apostle to the Jews of the dispersion.

8. What failures and faults occurred in this life?
   Peter—Impetuous nature; doubted Jesus' power; rebuked Christ for speaking of His death; denied Christ at His trial; resisted the vision of the Lord; changed face before the Jews at Antioch; tended to act first and think later.

9. What important contributions were made?
   Peter—introduced Jerusalem to the Christian Church; presented the gospel to Gentiles; wrote two epistles.

10. What one lesson is there in this life for you?
    Peter—His life illustrates the power of Jesus to transform lives from instability to strength.

11. What was the influence of the locality, geographically and historically?
    Peter—A rugged fisherman became a rugged preacher.

12. If this man were in our present society, what would be his occupational status?
    Peter—A missionary evangelist or great preacher and leader of men to Christ.

THE DIAGRAMMATIC METHOD/ John 1:1-18

1. *In the beginning was the Word,*
     and the Word was with God,
        and the Word was God.
2. *He was in the beginning with God.*
3. *All things came into being through Him:*
        And apart from Him nothing came into being
4. *that has come into being. (4) In Him was life;*
        and the life was the light of men.
5. *And the light shines in the darkness;*
        and the darkness did not comprehend it.
6. *There came a man, sent from God,*
        whose name was John.
7. *He came for a witness,*
        that he might bear witness of the light,
        that all might believe through him.

8.   *He was not the light,*
       but came that he might bear witness of the light.

9.   *There was the true light which,*
       coming into the world,
         enlightens every man.

10.   *He was in the world,*
       and the world was made through Him,
       and the world did not know Him.

11.   *He came to His own,*
       and those who were His own did not receive Him.

12.   *But as many as received Him,*
       to them He gave the right to become children of God,
       even to those who believe in His name:

13.   *who were born*
       not of blood,
       nor of the will of the flesh,
       nor of the will of man,
       but of God.

14. *And the Word became flesh,*
    and dwelt among us,
    and we beheld His glory,
     glory as of the only begotten from the Father,
    full of grace and truth.

15. *John bore witness of Him,*
  and cried out, saying,
     "This was He of whom I said,
      'He who comes after me has a higher rank than I,
      for He existed before me.' "

16. *For of His fullness we have all received,*
  and grace upon grace,

17.   *For the law was given through Moses;*
     grace and truth were realized through Jesus Christ.

18. *No man has seen God at any time;*
  the only begotten God,
    who is in the bosom of the Father,
    He has explained Him.

THE RHETORICAL METHOD

The traditional meaning of rhetoric is that of public address. If we were to use the term in its traditional way, we would study the discourses in the Gospel of John. There are fourteen major discourses in the book.

1. The New Birth 3:1-21
2. The Water of Life 4:4-26
3. The Source of Life, and the Witnesses 5:19-47
4. The Sustainer of Life 6:26-59
5. The Fountain of Truth 7:14-29
6. The Light of the World 8:12-20
7. The True Object of Faith 8:21-30
8. The Spiritual Freedom and Descent 8:31-59
9. The Shepherd of the Flock 10:1-21
10. The Oneness of Christ with the Father 10:22-38
11. The Redeemer of the World 12:20-36
12. The Coming Separation 13:31—14:31
13. The Nature and Issues of Union with Christ 15:1-27
14. The Holy Spirit and the Future 16:1-33

The first twelve discourses contain public instruction. Christ presents Himself to the world as the ultimate reality. The last two involve private instruction. In these, Christ reveals Himself to the disciples as the eternal sufficiency.

A more modern use of the term "rhetoric" refers to the literary use of language. In studying a book from this point of view, there would be an interest in word imagery, symbolism, and special literary forms.

There are no parables as such in the Gospel of John but there is a wide use of imagery.

temple 2:19
birth 3:3
wind 3:8
bride 3:29
harvest 4:35
lamp 5:35
flowing water 7:37
night and day 9:4
shepherd 10
door and porter 10:7-9
vine 15:1-7

The repetition of phrases is very effective in the Gospel of John. We can illustrate this by noting the seven times the phrase "cometh down from heaven" is repeated as a solemn refrain in Chapter 6. Another illustration is the use of the phrase, "I am," which occurs twenty-four times.

The bread of life 6:35
The light of the world 8:12
The door of the sheep 10:7

The good shepherd 10:11
The resurrection and the life 11:25
The way, the truth, and the life 14:6
The true vine 15:1

The Messiah 4:26
The living bread from heaven 6:51
One that beareth witness of Myself 8:18
The door 10:9
The Son of God 10:36
Master, and Lord 13:13
A king 18:37

From above 8:23
Before Abraham 8:58
With you 13:33
That where I am 14:3
In the Father 14:10
The vine 15:5
Come into the world 16:28
Not alone 16:32
Where I am 17:24
Jesus 18:5

THE THEOLOGICAL METHOD

This method of Bible study seeks to discover what is said regarding a particular doctrine. The references to the concept may be collected, classified, and conclusions drawn. Consideration is given in this study to six doctrines as they appear in the Gospel of John.

A. God, the Father
"The Father" 1:14; 1:18; 3:35; 4:21; 4:23; 5:19; 5:20; 5:21; 5:22; 5:23; 5:26; 5:36; 5:37; 5:45; 6:27; 6:37; 6:44; 6:45; 6:46; 6:57; 8:18; 8:27; 10:15; 10:30; 10:36; 10:38; 12:49; 12:50; 13:1; 13:3; 14:6; 14:8; 14:10; 14:13; 14:16; 14:23; 14:24; 14:26; 14:28; 14:31; 15:9; 15:16; 15:26; 16:3; 16:15; 16:17; 16:23; 16:25; 16:26; 16:27; 16:28; 16:32.

"My Father" 2:16; 5:17; 5:18; 5:43; 6:32; 8:19; 8:38; 8:49; 8:54; 10:18; 10:25; 10:29; 10:37; 14:2; 14:7; 14:20; 14:23; 15:1; 15:8; 15:10; 15:15; 15:23; 15:24.

Some Conclusions from These References
1. Christ came to carry out the Father's will (5:19, 36; 16:15).

2. Christ is one with the Father (6:57; 8:29; 10:30; 14:6).
3. The Father loved the Son (3:35; 5:20).
4. The Father must draw a person to the Son (6:44; 14:6).
5. The Father is to be glorified (14:13).
6. The Father answers prayer (15:16).

B. *The Deity of Christ*
John's portrait of Christ is fuller, more subtle, and indicates a
closer intimacy than the Synoptic writers. John deals with His
person. Matthew and Luke deal with His offices.

Jesus Speaks of Himself
    6:35 Bread of life
    8:12 Light of the world
   10:7 Door of the sheep
  10:11 The good shepherd
  11:25 Resurrection and the life
  14:6 The way, truth and life
  15:1 The true vine
Chapters which Emphasize His Deity
    1:49 Nathanael's testimony
    2:11 Miracle of Cana
    3:16 Word to Nicodemus
    4:26 Samaritan woman
    5:25 Impotent man
    6:33 Bread of life
    7:37 Water of life
    8:58 Light of the world
    9:37 Blind man
  10:30 The noble shepherd
  11:27 Martha's confession
  12:32 The Greeks
  13:31, 32 The supper
  14:1 Seeing the Father
  15:5 The vine and branches
  16:7 The Holy Spirit
  17:1 The prayer chapter
  18:1—19:16
  19:17-42
  20:28 The resurrection chapter
  21:4
  21:22 The seaside chapter
The Prologue (1:1-18)
    1:1 Christ is the word

1:4   Christ is the life
1:7   Christ is the light
1:18 Christ is the Son

Christ is Equal with God

5:19 In working
5:20 In knowing
5:23 In honor
5:22, 27 In judging
5:26 In self-existence

Jesus Bears Witness of Himself

8:12 He is the giver of light
8:36 He is the giver of liberty
8:51 He is the giver of life

Christ's Words in John's Gospel

In John's Gospel there are 879 verses (King James Version) or 866 (Revised Standard Version), and 419 of these contain words of our Lord, nearly half the Gospel. The number of verses in whole or part in the various chapters, which record His words, are as follows:

Chapter	Number of verses
1	8
2	5
3	17
4	20
5	33
6	37
7	17
8	40
9	8
10	29
11	17
12	20
13	22
14	28
15	27
16	29
17	26
18	11
19, 20	5-10
21	10

C. *The Holy Spirit*
1. He functions among believers only.
   14:17

15:27
14:23 (implied)
2. His function is to carry on the work of Jesus.
14:12
3. His function is to glorify the Son.
16:14
15:26
4. His function is to guide into all truth.
16:13
14:17; 15:26; 16:13
14:26
5. His function is to announce.
16:13, 14, 15
14:26
15:26, 27
6. His function is to convict the world.
16:8-11
14:17
7. His function is to make prayer real.
14:13-17
15:7
16:23, 24
8. His function is to make alive.
3:6, 7
6:63

Conclusions:
The Holy Spirit came from heaven (1:32).
The Holy Spirit marked Christ as the Son of God (1:33).
The Holy Spirit is the comforter (15:26).
Spiritual rebirth is necessary for eternal life (3:5).
The Spirit is unexplainable (3:8).
God is Spirit (4:24).
Jesus must leave before the Spirit comes (7:39).
The Holy Spirit comes from God, but is bestowed upon us as
    we receive the blessing of Christ (20:22).

D. The Miracles (Signs) in John
There are thirty-five miracles recorded by the four Gospel
writers. Nine of these are found in the Gospel of John. Seven
transpired before His death and one after His death. The
resurrection of Christ was the miracle climaxing all of the others.
Six of these are peculiar to the Gospel of John. They are the
ones reported in 2:1-11; 4:46-54; 5:1-9; 9:1-7; 11:17-44; and

21:1-14. The feeding of the 5,000 is recorded in John 6:1-14; Matt. 14; Mark 6; and Luke 9. Walking on the sea is recorded in John 6:16-21; Mark 6; and Matt. 14.

Many other signs therefore Jesus also performed in the presence of the disciples. which are not written in this book; but these have been written that you may believe that Jesus is the Christ, the Son of God; and that believing you may have life in His name. [John 20:30, 31]

	Miracle	Need Met	Jesus was Master Over
2:1-12	Water to wine	Social need	Nature and quality
4:46-54	Nobleman's son healed	Parental sorrow	Distance and disease
5:1-18	Impotent man healed	Physical need	Sin, time, and disease
6:1-14	Feeding the five thousand	Hunger	Material substance
6:15-21	Walking on the sea	Fear	Force of gravity
9:1-41	Blind man healed	Fate	Forces of nature (Destiny)
11:1-44	Raising of Lazarus	Sorrow	Death

Other sign verses:
2:11; 2:18; 2:23; 3:2; 4:48; 4:50; 4:54; 5:8; 6:2; 6:14; 6:19; 6:26; 6:30; 7:31; 9:7; 9:16; 10:41; 11:44; 11:47; 12:18; 12:37; 20:30; 21:6

E. Eternal Life in John's Gospel
1. And as Moses lifted up the serpent in the wilderness, even so must the Son of Man be lifted up; that whoever believes may in Him have eternal life (3:14, 15).
2. For God so loved the world, that He gave His only begotten Son, that whoever believes in Him should not perish, but have eternal life (3:16).
3. Already he who reaps is receiving wages, and is gathering fruit for life eternal (4:36).
4. You search the Scriptures, because you think that in them you have eternal life (5:39).
5. He who eats My flesh and drinks My blood has eternal life (6:54).
6. You have words of eternal life (6:68).
7. I give eternal life to them; and they shall never perish, and no one shall snatch them out of My hand (10:28).
8. He who loves his life loses it; and he who hates his life in this world shall keep it to life eternal (12:25).

9. Even as Thou gavest Him authority over all mankind, that to all whom Thou hast given Him, He may give eternal life (17:2).
10. And this is eternal life, that they may know Thee the only true God, and Jesus Christ whom Thou hast sent (17:3).

F. The Resurrection
The resurrection comes as a fulfillment of Christ's own prophecy recorded in John 2:19, in which He stated that He would raise the temple of His body after three days. This resurrection was to lead to convinced belief on the part of the disciples (John 2:22).

Four of the eleven appearances of Christ after the resurrection are recorded in the Gospel of John: 20:19-24; 20:26-29; 21:5, 6; and 21:15-17.

The Gospel of John includes several proofs of the resurrection. Some of these involved Mary Magdalene. She saw the stone rolled away, met the two angels, beheld the appearance of Christ, and carried on a conversation with Him. Peter and John saw the grave clothes, the napkin folded and separated from them, and the two appearances in the room. There were special witnesses including the angels and Thomas. The resurrection body itself was a proof. The Gospel account assures the reader of the fact that the body of Christ was not carried away by man. This was because of the arrangement of the grave clothes.

THE TOPICAL METHOD

"Believe" in the Gospel of John
I. Belief vs. Unbelief
2:11 "And His disciples believed in Him."
4:39 "Many of the Samaritans believed in Him."
4:50 "The man believed the word that Jesus spoke . . ."
6:69 "And we have believed . . ."
9:38 "And he said, 'Lord, I believe.' "
10:42 "And many believed in Him there."
11:45 "Many therefore of the Jews . . . believed in Him."
12:11 "Many of the Jews . . . were believing in Jesus."
12:42 "Nevertheless many even of the rulers believed in Him . . ."
Belief then decreases until the time of the resurrection when it rises again.

II. "Believe" occurs about 98 times

    1:7   "He came for a witness . . . that all might believe
        through him" (John the Baptist).

    1:12   "He gave the right to become children of God, even
        to those who believe in His name."

    1:50   Jesus to Nathanael: "Because I said to you that I saw
        you under the fig tree, do you believe?"

    2:11   "His disciples believed in Him."

    2:22   "They believed the Scripture . . ." (disciples).

    2:23   "Many believed in His name . . ."

    3:12   Jesus to Nicodemus: "If I told you earthly things
        and you do not believe, how shall you believe if I tell
        you heavenly things?"

    3:15   "Whoever believes may in Him have eternal life."

    3:16   "Whoever believes in Him should not perish, but
        have eternal life."

    3:18   "He who believes in Him is not judged."

    3:36   "He who believes in the Son has eternal life."

    4:21   Jesus to Samaritan woman: "Woman, believe Me,
        an hour is coming . . ."

    4:39   "Many of the Samaritans believed in Him . . ."

    4:41   "And many more believed because of His word."

    4:42   Samaritans to the woman: "It is no longer because
        of what you said that we believe . . ."

    4:48   "Unless you people see signs and wonders, you
        simply will not believe."

    4:50   "The man believed the word that Jesus spoke to
        him."

    4:53   "And he himself believed, and his whole
        household."

    5:24   "He who hears My word, and believes Him who
        sent Me, has eternal life . . ."

    5:38   "You do not believe Him whom He sent."

    5:44   "How can you believe, when you receive glory from
        one another . . ."

    5:46   "For if you believed Moses, you would believe Me."

    5:47   "But if you do not believe his writings, how will
        you believe My words?"

    6:29   "This is the work of God, that you believe in Him
        whom He has sent."

    6:30   "What then do You do for a sign, that we may see,
        and believe You?"

    6:35   "He who believes in Me shall never thirst."

6:36 "You have seen Me, and yet do not believe."

6:40 "Every one who beholds the Son, and believes in Him, may have eternal life."

6:47 "He who believes has eternal life."

6:64 "But there are some of you who do not believe."

6:69 "And we have believed and have come to know that You are the Holy One of God."

7:5 "For not even His brothers were believing in Him."

7:31 "But many of the multitude believed in Him."

7:38 "He who believes in Me, as the Scripture said, 'From his innermost being shall flow rivers of living water.'"

7:39 "But this He spoke of the Spirit, whom those who believed in Him were to receive."

7:48 "No one of the rulers or Pharisees has believed in Him, has he?"

8:24 "Unless you believe that I am He, you shall die in your sins."

8:30 "As He spoke these things, many came to believe in Him."

8:31 "Jesus therefore was saying to those Jews who had believed in Him . . ."

8:45 "But because I speak the truth, you do not believe Me."

8:46 "If I speak truth, why do you not believe Me?"

9:18 "The Jews therefore did not believe it of him . . ."

9:35 "Do you believe in the Son of Man?"

9:36 "And who is He, Lord, that I might believe in Him?"

9:38 "Lord, I believe."

10:25 "You do not believe; the works that I do in My Father's name . . ."

10:26 "But you do not believe, because you are not of My sheep."

10:37 "If I do not do the works of My Father, do not believe Me."

10:38 "Though you do not believe Me, believe the works."

10:42 "And many believed in Him there."

11:15 "And I am glad for your sakes that I was not there, so that you may believe."

11:25 "He who believes in Me shall live even if he dies."

11:26 "And everyone who lives and believes in Me shall never die. Do you believe this?"

11:27 "Yes, Lord, I have believed that You are the Christ."

11:40 "Did I not say to you, if you believe, you will see the glory of God?"

11:42 "That they may believe that Thou didst send Me."

11:45 "Many therefore of the Jews . . . believed in Him."

11:48 "All men will believe in Him . . ."

12:11 "Many of the Jews . . . were believing in Jesus."

12:36 "While you have the light, believe in the light . . ."

12:37 "Yet they were not believing in Him."

12:38 "Lord, who has believed our report?"

12:39 "For this cause they could not believe . . ."

12:42 "Many even of the rulers believed in Him . . ."

12:44 "He who believes in Me does not believe in Me, but in Him who sent Me."

12:46 "Everyone who believes in Me may not remain in darkness."

12:47 "And if any man hear my words, and believe not . . ." (KJV).

13:19 "You may believe that I am He."

14:1 "Believe in God, believe also in Me."

14:10 "Do you not believe that I am in the Father, and the Father is in Me?"

14:11 "Believe Me that I am in the Father, and the Father in Me; otherwise believe on account of the works themselves."

14:12 "He who believes in Me, the works that I do shall he do also."

14:29 "That when it comes to pass, you may believe."

16:9 "Concerning sin, because they do not believe in Me."

16:27 "You . . . have believed that I came forth from the Father."

16:30 "By this we believe that You came from God."

16:31 "Do you now believe?"

17:8 "They believed that Thou didst send Me."

17:20 "I do not ask in behalf of these alone, but for those also who believe in Me through their word."

17:21 "That the world may believe that Thou didst send Me."

19:35 "He knows that he is telling the truth, so that you also may believe."

20:8 "He saw, and believed."

20:25 "I will not believe."
20:29 "Because you have seen Me, have you believed? Blessed are they who did not see, and yet believed."
20:31 "But these have been written that you may believe that Jesus is the Christ, the Son of God; and that believing you may have life in His name."

III. Belief and Unbelief
   A. Nature of Belief
      1. Strong feeling—demands affections; demands facts (6:69)
      2. Assent to claims (6:29)
      3. Experiential knowledge (4:42)
      4. Worship (9:38; 20:29)
      5. Receiving (1:12)
      6. Acceptance (3:18)
   B. Cause of Belief
      1. Testimony of the Father and others
      2. Works
      3. Experience
   C. Results of Belief
      1. Sonship
      2. Eternal life
      3. Spirit
      4. Quenching Thirst
      5. Abiding presence
      6. Removal of judgment
   D. Causes of Unbelief
      1. Ignorance—Nathanael
      2. Jealousy—Jews
      3. Ambition—Judas
      4. Materialism—multitude
      5. Pessimism and sorrow
      6. Nationalism
      7. Prejudice
      8. Expediency
      9. Pride
    10. Fear
   E. Results of Unbelief
      1. Failure—Judas
      2. Condemnation (3:18)
      3. Death (8:21)
      4. Conviction of sin (16:9)

      5. Breaking of fellowship
      6. Hardness
      7. Rejection and the cross
         The great paradox—Sin leads to the cross, but
         only the cross can take away sin.
   F. There is a rising progression in belief in chapters
     1—12

"Witness" in the Gospel of John
A. The Greek *verb marturein* meaning *"to witness"* is found
   thirty-three times in the Gospel of John and thirty times in
   the rest of the New Testament. The English verb "to
   witness" can be seen in the following verses:
   John 1:7, 8, 15, 32, 34; 2:25; 3:11, 26, 28, 32; 4:39, 44; 5:31,
   32, 33, 36, 37, 39; 7:7; 8:13, 14, 18; 10:25; 12:17; 13:21; 15:26,
   27; 18:23, 37; 19:35; 21:24
B. The *noun "witness"* in the English text can be found in the
   following verses:
   John 1:7, 19; 3:11, 32, 33; 5:31, 32, 34, 36; 8:13, 14, 17; 19:35;
   21:24
C. *Several types of witness appear in the Gospel of John.*
    1. There is the witness of *John the Baptist.*
       1:7, 8, 15, 19, 32, 34; 3:26; 5:32, 33, 35
    2. There is the witness of *Christ.*
       3:11, 32; 4:44; 5:31, 32, 34, 36, 37, 39; 7:7; 8:13, 14, 17, 18;
       10:25; 13:21; 18:37
    3. There is the witness of *Scripture.*
       John 5:39, 40, 46
    4. There is the witness of the *Holy Spirit.*
       John 3:11; 15:26; 16:13, 14
    5. There is the witness of the *Father.*
       John 5:31, 32, 34, 37; 8:18
    6. There is the witness of *Christ's works.*
       John 5: 17, 36; 10:25; 14:11; 15:25, 26
    7. There is the witness of the *woman of Samaria.*
       John 4:39
    8. There is the witness of the *people or multitude.*
       John 3:28; 12:17
    9. There is the witness of the *disciples.*
       John 15:27; 19:35; 21:24

Whether we regard the sublimity of its thought, the width and spirituality of its conception of religion, the depth of its moral insight, or the tragic pathos of its story, we cannot but feel that we have before us the work of a master mind. And when we remember how it has moulded the faith and touched the heart and calmed the sorrows of generations of men, we must approach it with orderly reverence, and with a desire to penetrate its inmost meaning and become more thoroughly imbued with its kindling power.

JAMES DRUMMOND *An Inquiry into the Character and Authorship of the Fourth Gospel* (London: Williams and Norgate for the Hibbert Trustees, 1903), p. 1.

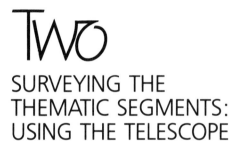

Two

SURVEYING THE THEMATIC SEGMENTS: USING THE TELESCOPE

LOCATING THE SEGMENTS

OUTLINING THE SEGMENTS

1:1-18 Prologue: The Word Became Flesh
   1:1-5   The Revelation of the Word
   1:6-11 The Rejection of the Word
   1:2-18 The Reception of the Word

1:19-51 Bearing Witness
   1:19-28 The Witness of John the Baptist
   1:29-34 The Lamb of God (1:36; Acts 8:32; 1 Peter 1:19)
   1:35-51 The witness to the first disciples
    35-39 Through the preached Word
    40-42 Through personal influence
    43   Through direct appeal
    45, 46 Through personal testimony

2:1-11 Christ's First Miracle
   2:1, 2   The place
   2:3-5   The problem
   2:6-8   The plan
   2:9-11   The product

2:12-22 The Cleansing Christ
   2:12-16 Cleansing the old temple
   2:17-22 Announcing the new temple
     Doubtful rejoinder (18, 20, 21)
     Faithful reminder (22)

2:23—3:21 A Midnight Interview
   2:23—3:2 The divine disclosure: *Announcement of the new messenger*
   3:3-15   The divine demand: *Statement of the new birth*
    3:3   The necessity of the new birth
    3:7, 8   The nature of the new birth

3:14, 15 The nearness of the new birth
3:16-21   The divine declaration: *Summary of the new birth*

3:22-36 Recessional and Processional
   3:22-30 Retiring address for himself—A man without envy
            (v. 29)
   3:31-36 Inaugural address for Christ—A gift without
            measure (v. 34)

4:1-42 Witnessing When Weary
   4:1-30 Witnessing to the woman
           4:1-6   Convenience
           4:7-15   Curiosity
           4:16-26 Confrontation
           4:27-30 Commitment
   4:31-38 Witnessing to the disciples
           4:31-34 Satisfying food
           4:35-38 Rejoicing together
   4:39-42 Witnessing to the Samaritans
           4:39 The word of the woman
           4:41 The word of the Savior

4:43-54 Growing a Great Faith
   4:43-47 The bequest of faith
           (A great sorrow)
   4:48-50 The test of faith
           (A great Savior)
   4:51-54 The reward of faith
           (A great satisfaction)

5:1-18 The Healing Christ
   5:1-9   The contact—helplessness and hope
           5:1-5 Jesus seeks out His man
           5:6-9 Jesus deals with His man
   5:10-18 The controversy—healing and hatred
           5:10-16 Breaking Sabbath
           5:17, 18 Speaking blasphemy

5:19-47 The Unique Christ
   5:19-29 Amazing claims
           5:19, 20 Observes the faith
           5:21   Gives life
           5:22   Pronounces judgment

          5:23   Deserves honor
          5:24-29 Summons the dead
   5:30-47 Assuring confirmations
          5:30-35 Confirmation by John
          5:36   Confirmation by works
          5:37, 38 Confirmation by the Father
          5:39, 40 Confirmation of the Word
          5:41-47 Four calls to believe
          5:41, 42 The love of God
          5:43   The name of the Father
          5:44   The glory of God
          5:45-47 The writings of Moses

6:1-21 Popularity at Its Peak
   6:1-14 Food for five thousand
          6:1-4 The people
          6:5-7 The problem
          6:8-14 The provision
   6:15-21 Walking on water
          6:15-19 His presence
          6:20, 21 His peace

6:22-71 Reactions to a Great Message (Discourse on the Bread of Life)
   6:22-40 The multitude: "What shall we do that we may work the works of God?" ("What should we do?")
   6:41-59 The Jews: "Is not this Jesus, the son of Joseph, whose father and mother we know? How does He now say, 'I have come down out of heaven?' " ("Don't we know him?")
   6:60-71 The disciples: "This is a difficult statement; who can listen to it?" ("Who can understand him?")

7:1-13 The Misunderstood Christ
   7:1-9   The unbelief of the brethren: Departure
   7:10-13 The bewilderment of the multitude: Division

7:14-36 Marveling at the Master
   7:14-18 Justification of His creed   } 7:14-24
   7:19-24 Justification of His conduct J The controversy
   7:25-36 Justification of His commission 7:25-36
                                  The conflict

7:37-52 *If Any Man Thirst*
    7:37-44 The Fountain of living water
          7:37, 38 The condition
                    The command
                    The compensation
                    The supposition
                    The invitation
                    The prescription
                    The culmination
    7:45-52 Identified by His speech

7:53—8:11 *Set Free by the Savior* or *A Miserable Sinner and*
          Merciful Savior
    7:53—8:6 The case for the prosecution
    8:7-11   The case for the defense

8:12-30 *The Witness of the "I Am"*
    8:12-16 I am the light of the world
    8:17-20 I am the one who bears witness
    8:21-26 I am from above
    8:27-30 I am the Son of Man

8:31-59 *A Discourse of Discernment*
    8:31-36 Discerning the true disciples
              Abiding in Christ's Word
              Knowing Christ's truth
              Possessing Christ's freedom
    8:37-42 Discerning Nominal Children
              Have no place for Christ's Word
              Have a wicked life
              Have no love for Christ
    8:43-47 Discerning the real enemies
              Cannot understand Christ's Word
              Offspring of Satan
              Do not believe the truth
    8:48-59 Discerning Christ's true nature
              Glorifies the Father
              Protects from death
              Receives glory
              Knows the Father
              Lives forever

9:1-41 Light for Blind Eyes
   9:1-5   The case
              The condition
              The consideration given:
                by the Disciples 9:2
                by the Neighbors 9:8
                by the Pharisees 9:13-16
   9:6-24 The cure
              The preparation
              The process
   9:25-41 The consequences
              Testimony
                positive
                personal
                public
              Trial

10:1-21 The New Testament's Twenty-Third Psalm
   10:1-6   The fold and the flock
   10:7-10   The door
   10:11-21 The Shepherd
               Relinquishes His life
               Recognizes His sheep
               Reassembles the flock
               Reclaims His life

10:22-42 Great Affirmations: I and the Father
   10:22-30 Jesus affirms His deity in response to the
              questioning of the Jews
   10:31-38 Jesus argues His claims in response to the
              threatening of the Jews
   10:39-42 Jesus alludes their grasp in response to the force
              of the Jews

11:1-53 The Resurrection and the Life
   11:1-27   The prelude to the raising of Lazarus
              11:1-16 The great problem
              11:17-27 The great revelation
   11:28-53 The account of the raising of Lazarus
              11:28-37 The great sorrow
              11:38-44 The great victory
               11:45-53 The great dilemma

11:54—12:11 Love's Extravagance
    11:54-57 Turning from a public to a private ministry
    12:1-11   More than supper
              The act of Mary
              The attitude of Judas

12:12-50 The Coming King
    12:12-19 The triumphal entry
              Royal greeting (12, 13)
              Ancient prophecy (14-16)
              Living witness (17-19)
    12:20-36 The divided response
              12:20-26 A paradox for pondering
                        Three Greeks and Philip
                        The seed and death
                        Service and honor
              12:27-36 Through trouble to triumph
                        Troubled (27-30)
                        Exalted (31-34)
                        Believed (35, 36)
    12:37-50 The Inescapable Judgment
              37-41 The prediction of the prophet
              42,43 The pressure of society
              44-50 The power of the Word

13:1-30 The Royalty of Service
    13:1-11   The example of washing the disciple's feet
    13:12-17 The explanation of the example
    13:18-30 The expulsion of the traitor

13:31—14:31 Glory By and By
    13:31-38 Jesus is departing
              13:31-33 A statement
              13:34,35 A command
              13:36-38 A warning
    14:1-6   A discussion of destiny
    14:7-11   A disclosure of God
    14:12-31 Promises unlimited
              New power 14:12
              New prayer 14:13, 14
              New presence 14:16, 17
              New peace 14:27-31

15:1-27 Rewarding Relationships
15:1-8   The revealing of the relationship
15:9-17   The rewards of the relationship
15:18-27 The reactions to the relationship

16:1-33 Words of Courage
16:1-4a   Enduring persecution
16:4b-15 The work of the Holy Spirit
       16:4b-7   The benefit of His coming
       16:8-11   Convicting the world
       16:12-15 Teaching believers
16:16-33 The encouraging farewell
       16:16-23a You will see me
       16:23b-33 The Father loves you

17:1-26 Praying to the Father
17:1-5   Glorification of the Son
17:6-19   Preservation of the disciples
17:20-26 Unity of all believers

18:1-27 A Study in Contrasts
18:1-11   Confession and denial
18:12-27 Meekness and fear

18:28—19:16 The King of the Jews
18:28-40 His heavenly kingdom
19:1-16   His superior authority

19:17-42 The Lamb of God
19:17-22 Exaltation
19:23-27 Intercession
19:28-37 Fulfillment
19:38-42 Entombment

20:1-31 Christ Is Risen
20:1-10   Impressions at the empty tomb
       20:1-3   Sorrow
       20:4-7   Perplexity
       20:8-10   Belief
20:11-29 The power of the resurrection
       20:11-18 Sorrow dispelled
       20:19-23 Perplexity removed
       20:24-31 Belief affirmed

21:1-25 You follow me!
   21:1-14   A new concern
   21:15-19 A new commission
   21:20-25 A new consideration

SYNTHESIZING THE SEGMENTS

THEME: The Son of God, The Son of Man
1. Revealing the Son of God   John 1-12
   a. Witness to the Word made flesh
      Chapter 1
   b. Believing the works and words of Christ
      Chapter 2—4
   c. The announcements of Christ at the Jewish feasts
      Chapters 5—10
   d. The climax of Christ's public ministry
      Chapters 11—12

2. Glorifying the Son of Man   John 13—21
   a. The Words of Christ for troubled disciples
      Chapters 13—17
   b. The World's response to the King of the Jews
      Chapters 18—20
   c. The Risen Shepherd cares for His sheep
      Chapter 21

THEME: Christ and His Ministry
1. Prologue (1:1-18)
   a. Relation of the Word to God (1:1, 2)
   b. Relation of the Word to creation (1:3)
   c. Relation of the Word to mankind (1:4-13)
   d. Incarnation of the Word (1:14-18)

2. Christ in His Public Ministry (1:19—12:50)
   a. The Testimony of John the Baptist (1:19-34)
   b. The Testimony of Jesus' first disciples (1:35-51)
   c. The Testimony of the first sign (2:1-11)
   d. The Manifestation of Christ in Jerusalem and Judea
      (2:12—3:36)
   e. The Manifestation of Christ to the woman of Samaria
      (4:1-42)
   f. The Manifestation of Christ to the nobleman in Galilee
      (4:43-54)

g. The healing of the impotent man and subsequent controversy (5:1-47)
h. The Bread of Life (6:1-71)
i. Christ at the Feast of Tabernacles (7:1-52)
j. The woman taken in adultery (7:53—8:11)
k. Jesus the light of the world (8:12-59)
l. The healing of the man born blind (9:1-41)
m. The discourse of the Good Shepherd (10:1-21)
n. Events of the Feast of Dedication (10:22-42)
o. The raising of Lazarus (11:1-57)
p. Jesus' triumphal entry into Jerusalem (12:1-50)

3. Christ in His Private Ministry to the Disciples (13:1—17:26)
a. Washing the disciples' feet (13:1-17)
b. Jesus foretells His betrayal (13:18-32)
c. The new commandment (13:33-35)
d. Jesus foretells Peter's denial (13:36-38)
e. The comforting Christ (14:1-31)
f. Instruction regarding the believer's relationships (15:1-27)
g. Declaration of coming events (16:1-33)
h. The high priestly prayer of Jesus (17:1-26)

4. Christ in His Passion Ministry (18:1—20:31)
a. The arrest of Jesus (18:1-11)
b. The trial before the high priest (18:12-27)
c. The trial before Pilate (18:28—19:16)
d. The crucifixion and burial of Jesus (19:17-42)
e. The resurrection of Christ (20:1-29)
f. Jesus and the signs (20:30, 31)

5. Epilogue (21:1-25)
a. Jesus is the source of the disciples' needs for service (21:1-14)
b. The public restoration of Peter (21:15-19)
c. Conclusion (21:20-25)

THEME: *The Revelation of Jesus as the Son of God*
1. Prologue (1:1-18)
a. The Word was God (1:1-3)
b. The Word became flesh (1:4-18)

2. Revelaton to the Jews (1:19—12:50)
a. John's testimony (1:19-28)
b. Jesus acclaimed Son of God (1:29-42)

    c. Philip and Nathanael (1:43-51)
    d. Marriage in Cana (2:1-12)
    e. Cleansing of the temple (2:13-22)
    f. Nicodemus (3:1-15)
    g. The Baptist's final testimony (3:22-30)
    h. Witness of heaven (3:31-36)
    i. Woman of Samaria (4:1-38)
    j. The nobleman's son cured (4:46-54)
    k. The cure at Bethesda (5:1-18)
    l. Jesus testifies of His connection with the Father (5:18-47)
    m. Feeding the five thousand (6:1-14)
    n. Jesus walks on the sea (6:14-20)
    o. Jesus the bread of life (6:21-59)
    p. Peter's testimony (6:66-71)
    q. Jews seek Jesus (7:1-13)
    r. Jesus' testimony (7:25-44)
    s. The officer's testimony (7:45-52)
    t. The woman in adultery (8:1-12)
    u. Jesus the light of the world (8:12-30)
    v. Jesus sent from the Father (8:31-59)
    w. The Pharisees examine Jesus (9:1-41)
    x. Jesus the Good Shepherd (10)
    y. Raising of Lazarus (11)
    z. Lazarus, Martha, and Mary (12:1-11)
    aa. Triumphal entry (12:12-20)
    bb. The last discourse of Jesus (12:20-50)

3. Revelation to the Disciples (13:1—19:42)
    a. Jesus sums up His claims (13)
    b. The Second Coming (14)
    c. A Christian must be of Christ (15)
    d. Courage to the disciples (16)

4. Revelation through His Passion (18:1—19:42)

5. His Resurrection and Appearance (20:1—21:25)

John, as if it oppressed him to walk on earth, has opened his words as it were with a burst of thunder, has lifted himself not only above earth and every sphere of sky and heaven, but even above every host of angels, and every order of invisible powers, and reaches to Him by whom all things were made, as he says, "In the beginning was the Word. . . ." He proclaims other things in keeping with this great sublimity with which he begins, and speaks of the divinity of our Lord as no other person has spoken. He pours forth that into which he had drunk. For not without reason is it mentioned in his own Gospel, that at the feast he reclined upon the bosom of his Lord. From that bosom he had in secrecy drunk in the stream, but what he drank in secret he poured forth openly.

AURELIUS AUGUSTINE Bishop of Hippo, *Tractates on the Gospel According to St. John,* tract. 36, chap. 8, pg 1.

Three

STUDYING UNIQUE FEATURES OF THE CONTENT: USING THE MICROSCOPE

One of the outstanding characteristics of the Gospel of John is its simplicity of expression. It is easier to read the Greek text of this Gospel than that of any of the others. It has a remarkable combination of clearness and profundity of revelation. One writer has likened it to the waters of Lake Tahoe—crystal clear but of unfathomable depths. It is as simple as a child and as sublime as a seraph. It is as gentle as a lamb and bold as an eagle.

John had a remarkable literary style. There was first of all a fondness for choice words. Such words as believe, world, life, witness, glory, name, behold, work, sign, darkness, and flesh seemed to be outstanding in his vocabulary. Just as there was a stress upon the choice of words, so there was on the choice of ideas and their repetition. For instance, when the relatives are brought into view, then something was said about his "hour." When Judas appeared, his betrayal is recalled and something is also said at that point about Satan. When John the Baptist came into view, then there was reference to his witness. The parallelism of Hebrew poetry is apparent in such double sentences as "Peace I leave with you; my peace I give unto you" (14:27). There are several Hebraistic forms of expression. Twenty-five times in this Gospel and nowhere else in the New Testament we find Christ beginning His speech with a "Verily, verily," which is in Hebrew "Amen, amen."

The many unique words and phrases demand that we not only look at the Gospel of John through a telescope which will point out the generalities. We must also look at the Gospel through a microscope and see the minute features of style.

JOHN 1:1-18

Who?

1. God

    He made all things.

    He was not seen by man but was declared by Christ.

    He is the supreme ruler of the world and the one true God.

    God is Spirit, infinite, eternal, and unchangeable in His being.

    Wisdom, power, justice, goodness, truth, and love are His attributes.

2. John

    He was sent from God as a witness of the Light.

    Elizabeth and Zacharias were his parents.

    His birth was foretold by Gabriel.

    He was born six months before Christ.

    He was a Nazarite from his birth.

    When he was twenty years of age, he went into the desert for ten years.

    He was beheaded as a result of the intrigue of Herodius.

3. Moses

    He was born in Goshen, Egypt, about 1571 B.C.

    He was shielded from the wrath of Pharoah and lived forty years in Egypt.

    He died on Mount Nebo.

4. Christ

    He was born of the Virgin Mary, God being His Father.

When?

No time is given.

Where?

No place is listed.

Why?

This passage was given to introduce the eternal incarnate Word.

What?

This is the prologue which sets the thematic foundation for the entire Gospel.

Wherefore?

The ministry of John the Baptist was established.

Jesus Christ is established as the Light of the world.

Content Comments

1:1   IN THE BEGINNING—A reference to time before creation, an allusion to Genesis one with common ideas of creation, life, light, and darkness. "Beginning" here refers to the period before creation.

1:1   WAS—A reference to the eternal existence of the Word, in contrast to verse 3, "came into being."

1:1   THE WORD—The Greek use of *Logos* (Word) as a principle or force, as the rationality of the universe would make this term important and meaningful to a Greek reader. But the Jewish background reflects more appropriately the ideas developed by John: God spoke in creation; the Word of the Lord came to the prophets; the Law is the word of the Lord; and wisdom is a near personification, as in Proverbs 8. The New Testament uses *logos* (word) as a synonym for "gospel" (Mark 2:2, Acts 10:44; and 1 Thess. 1:6). John gives full expression to these developments of thought by the climactic declaration that the Word is a living person who was the agency of creation and gives life to men. Only in John 1:1 and 1:14 is "Word" so used, though Revelation 19:13 is remarkably similar. The rest of the Gospel emphasizes the word(s) of Jesus as being the word(s) of God.

1:1   WITH—Literally "toward" emphasizing relationship or accompaniment.

1:1   WAS GOD—John here asserts that the Word was God; it is not an adjective ("divine") nor indefinite ("a god").

1:2   HE—Literally "this one." The emphasis is upon the same Word mentioned in verse 1.

1:3   THAT HAS COME INTO BEING—This may be the end of the sentence in verse 3, or it may be the beginning of the sentence in verse 4: "That which has come into being in Him was life."

1:4   LIFE—John regularly uses this word for eternal life; it occurs thirty-six times.

1:5   COMPREHEND—Or "overcome." John emphasizes the opposition between light and darkness, and uses the same verb in 12:35: ". . . that the darkness may not overtake you. . ." Verses 4 and 5 form a poem, with the last word of a line serving as the first word of the next line.

1:6   THERE CAME A MAN—This verse is in strong contrast to verse 1. This is the same word used in the Greek translation of

Genesis to describe creation. The man came into being, was created, but the Word always was.

1:6   A MAN—Literally "human" in contrast to the Word who was God.

1:7   WITNESS—This is an important idea in this Gospel. It occurs as a noun fourteen times and as a verb thirty-three times. Only the witness of John is mentioned, not his preaching, not his baptizing.

1:8   HE—Literally "that one." It emphasizes the distinction between John and the light.

1:8   NOT THE LIGHT—Jesus himself is the light (3:19; 8:12; 9:5) but John is a lamp (5:35).

1:9   TRUE—Two adjectives are used by John twenty-one times to stress the "authentic" and the "genuine."

1:10   WORLD—This word is used seventy-eight times in this Gospel. It is used to refer to the created world or universe, to mankind, and to the opponents of Christ. God loves and Jesus came to save the world (ch. 3).

1:11   HIS OWN—The first occurrence is neuter, referring to one's own possessions, such as home (19:27) or homeland (Israel, Jerusalem, the Promised Land); the second is masculine and refers to one's own people, here the Jewish nation. In Exodus 19:5, Israel is God's own possession.

1:12   HE GAVE THE RIGHT—It is a gift of privilege, a change of status.

1:12   TO BECOME—The same word used for creation of all things in verse 3 and the coming into existence of John (v. 6). This prologue is the narration of the *new* creation which climaxes in people becoming God's children.

1:12   CHILDREN—John uses the word "Son" of Jesus Christ only; believers are God's offspring, His children.

1:12   BELIEVE IN—To place complete confidence in Him, not merely to believe something He said or did. He is to be trusted entirely. Compare John 4:50 with 4:53. The tense of the verb emphasizes continuous believing.

1:12   HIS NAME—A representation of the person in all of His significance. Jewish naming of children was understood to be descriptive and predictive. Even more so is this true of "Jesus" the Savior.

1:13   BLOOD . . . WILL OF THE FLESH . . . WILL OF MAN—These three phrases strongly negate any human effort in the spiritual birth. The first refers to human procreation (the word is plural: "bloods"), the second refers to natural sexual desire, and the third refers to individual human decision.

1:14 THE WORD BECAME FLESH—The profound combination of the eternal Word of verse 1 and the man of verse 6, introduces the climactic section of the prologue.

1:14 DWELT—Literally "tented," perhaps a reference to the tabernacle of God among men. This verb is used only here and four times in Revelation.

1:14 GLORY—As the "Shekinah" glory of God was associated with the tabernacle, so the glory of God was seen by the human eye in the lowly manifestation of the incarnate Word.

1:14 ONLY BEGOTTEN—Literally "one of a kind," or, "unique." It is used of an only child as in Luke 7:12 and 8:42, for example.

1:14 GRACE AND TRUTH—Grace—God's undeserved favor which produces joy—occurs only these three times in the prologue. Truth is both the opposite of falsehood (8:45) and the very character of God and the Son (14:6).

1:15 BORE WITNESS—Literally "bears witness." The witness of John the Baptist continues to be effective: "He has shouted."

1:15 HE EXISTED BEFORE ME—This phrase is literally "He was first than me," indicating the absolute priority of the Word.

1:17 JESUS CHRIST—This is the first identification of the Word. His double name occurs only here and 17:3 in this Gospel. Compare 20:31. John uses the human name "Jesus" 237 times, more than any other NT writing.

1:18 ONLY BEGOTTEN GOD—This is a combination of the "unique (Son)" of verse 14 and "was God" of verse 1. Thus "the Unique One, who is God," is a climactic conclusion to the prologue.

1:18 HE HAS EXPLAINED—This verb is used of narratives and of revealing divine secrets. It suggests both completeness and revelation.

JOHN 1:19-51

Who?
1. John the Baptist
   Described in the prologue section.

2. Jews (Men of Judah)
   A member of the kingdom of Judah after the separation of
   the ten tribes. The name "Jew" in John's writings is
   used of those who were antagonistic toward the
   teachings of Jesus. They were the blind followers of
   the Pharisees.

3. Levites (The descendants of Levi)
   It usually refers to those of the tribe who were not priests.

4. Christ
   Described in the prologue section.

5. Elias (The Greek form for Elijah; My God is Jehovah)
   A Tishbite of the inhabitants of Gilead—The grandest and
   most romantic character that Israel ever produced.

6. Esaias (The Greek form for Isaiah)
   A prophet, the son of Amoz. The Hebrew name signifies
   "Jehovah is salvation." He prophesied concerning Judah
   and Jerusalem in the days of Uzziah, Jotham, Ahaz,
   and Hezekiah. He was the greatest of the prophets. He
   was a prophet-preacher, a man of genius in literary
   work, and a man of eloquence and wisdom.

7. Pharisees (Separated ones)
   A religious party or school among the Jews at the time of
   Christ. These were called the formalists. The group
   was founded just before the Maccabean War as a protest
   against the advancing Hellenistic influence. They
   stood for a strict observance of the Law. Their strictness
   led them to formulate a great variety of extra rules.

8. Israel
   The national name of the twelve tribes. It lasted 216
   years, from 937 to 721 B.C.

9. Holy Ghost
   The third member of the Trinity of the Godhead.

10. Andrew
    One of our Lord's Apostles. Brother of Simon Peter. He
    was of Bethsaida and was formerly connected with
    John the Baptist and then left him to follow Christ. He
    was placed fourth in importance among the disciples.
    It was said of him that he was crucified at Patrae in
    Achaia. He was quiet, approachable, friendly.

11. Simon Peter
    He was the son of Jonas. He was a fisherman and was the
    brother of Andrew. He was born in Bethsaida. He was

killed by crucifixion. One of the most intimate
disciples, he was weak natured, but Christ was going to
make him strong.

12. Philip

Born in Bethsaida. He was one of the earliest disciples to
be with the Lord. He was among the group of disciples at
Jerusalem after the ascension and on the Day of
Pentecost. He was stubborn.

13. Nathanael (God has given)

He was a disciple of Jesus and was born at Cana of Galilee. It
was Philip who first brought Nathanael to Christ. He
was skeptical.

What?

John makes known to his inquirers the fact that he is not the
Christ, but is rather the forerunner of Christ. He witnesses to
the fact that Jesus is the Lamb of God which taketh away the
sin of the world. Andrew, Philip, Peter, and Nathanael are
called to be disciples of Christ.

When?

In the year A.D. 27. It was the first year of Christ's ministry.

Where?

Jerusalem (The city of peace) (1:19)—The supreme city in the
world as to its influence upon the hopes and destiny of the
world. It is thirty-two miles from the sea, eighteen from
Jordan, twenty from Hebron, and thirty-six from Samaria. It
is situated on the top of a ridge of hills. It has almost no
commerce or business. It was the scene of the life, passion,
cross, and grave of Christ. The city has had many earthquakes
and has also undergone nearly twenty severe sieges.

Bathabara—Bethany; possibly Bethbarah (1:28). This is the
place where John baptized Jesus. It was an obscure village
near Bethabara and was fourteen miles below the Sea of
Galilee.

Bethsaida (House of fish) (1:44)—It was in the land of
Gennesareth. It was the place where the five thousand were
fed. There was a Bethsaida of Galilee and one of Julias
separated only by a small stream.

Nazareth (Offshoot) (1:45)—It was the ordinary residence of
our Savior. It is situated among the hills which constitute the
south ridges of Lebanon, just before the plain of Esdraelon. It
was a city of fifteen to twenty thousand people. It is within
the limits of the province of Galilee.

Why?
It is used to set forth the fact that John knew Christ to be the Lamb of God and so proclaimed Him. It gives the first reason for believing in His deity in that He takes away the sins of the world by being the Lamb of God. It thus introduces us to the main theme of the deity of Christ by giving the first basis for the thesis.

Wherefore?
John was the forerunner of Christ.
Jesus accepted four disciples.
Jesus' mission is set forth in that He was to take away the sins of the world.

Content Comments
1:19 THE JEWS—This term, used over seventy times in John, refers most often to the hostile religious persons, especially in Judea and Jerusalem.
1:19 PRIESTS AND LEVITES—An official embassy from Jerusalem. The Levites provided music and served as guards for the temple. They were Sadducees, concerned with ecclesiastical politics.
1:20 CONFESSED—Or "admitted." This triple statement (positive, negative, positive) occurs only here in John.
1:20 I—This emphatic pronoun occurs 465 times in this Gospel.
1:21 AND—Literally "therefore." This is John's favorite conjunction since he uses it 195 times in his Gospel.
1:24 PHARISEES—Represented the common people, with concern for pure religion.
1:27 NOT WORTHY TO UNTIE—Even though it was the task of a slave.
1:28 BETHANY—Not the town near Jerusalem, mentioned in 11:18. The location of this Bethany has not been determined.
1:29 LAMB OF GOD—Occurs four times in the NT: John 1:36; Acts 8:32; 1 Peter 1:19.
1:30 WHOM I SAID—This statement of John is not recorded in the Gospel.
1:30 A MAN—A reference to the full humanity of Jesus Christ.
1:31 ISRAEL—Unlike the expression "the Jews" this is a favorable term in John's Gospel, used four times: 1:49; 3:10; 12:13.
1:34 THE SON OF GOD—Or possibly "the chosen one of God."
1:35 TWO OF HIS DISCIPLES—The first was Andrew (v. 40), the second was likely John, the beloved disciple who does

not mention his own name. John's disciples concentrated on fasting and prayers (Luke 5:33; Mark 2:18).

1:38 RABBI—Literally "My Great One." John uses the word eight times, Matthew four, and Mark three times.

1:38 WHAT DO YOU SEEK?—The first words of Jesus in this Gospel, with meaning for the reader as well.

1:39 TENTH HOUR—Reckoned from daylight about 6 A.M. John characteristically notes such details as time: 4:6, 52; 18:28; 19:14; 20:19.

1:40 SIMON PETER—Occurs seventeen times in John but only three times in Matthew, twice in Luke and once in Mark. He was the better known of the two brothers.

1:41 FIRST—Most likely an adverb here: "before doing anything else."

1:42 CEPHAS—This Aramaic word meaning "Stone" is used only here by John and five times by Paul. A new name asserts the authority of the giver and new character to the recipient.

1:43 FOLLOW ME—John uses three words to indicate response to Jesus: "follow," "look," and "believe."

1:44 BETHSAIDA—"House of fishing." Their home town, though Peter and Andrew lived in Capernaum during the ministry of Jesus (Mark 1:21, 29).

1:45 NATHANAEL—"God has given." He has been identified with Simon the Cananaean (Mark 3:18) and with Bartholomew, though it is more likely that he was not one of the twelve.

1:45 SON OF JOSEPH—Jesus' legal or customary name, which distinguished him from other persons bearing the name "Yeshua."

1:46 ANYTHING GOOD—An indication of rivalry between the regions.

1:46 COME AND SEE—A phrase common to the rabbis and meaningful to the reader.

1:47 ISRAELITE INDEED—One who is worthy of the name. Used only here in John, eight times elsewhere in the NT.

1:47 GUILE—Originally was bait for fishing, then meant cunning or deceit.

1:48 HOW—Literally "Where did you know me?" So Jesus answers "Under the fig tree." It was a symbol of home, and peace, and a place of study, meditation, and prayer.

1:49 THE KING OF ISRAEL—An unusual phrase that occurs only four times in the NT: Here and 12:13; Matthew 27:42; and Mark 15:32.

1:51 TO HIM . . . TO YOU—Often in this Gospel there is a change
from the singular (him) to the plural (you all), indicating
that the answer to the individual is important for
everyone.

1:51 TRULY, TRULY—Or "Amen, amen." Only John reports the
double amen, and that twenty-five times. Only Jesus
used it as a prefix for a following statement.

1:51 HEAVEN OPENED—This represents communication between
heaven and earth. Compare 3:13, 3:31, 6:33, and 12:28.

1:51 SON OF MAN—Jesus' favorite title for Himself, used twelve
times in John (including 8:28). Cf. Ezekiel 2:1 and Daniel
7:13. Contrast "Son of Perdition" (17:12).

JOHN 2:1-11

Who?

1. Mary
   She was of the tribe of Judah and of the lineage of David.
   She is mentioned only four times after the beginning of
       Christ's ministry.
   She gives evidence of the fact that she recognized that Jesus
       was not an ordinary man.

2. Ruler of the Feast

3. Disciples

When?
The initial year of Christ's ministry.

What?
The account of a Jewish wedding feast in Cana.

Where?
At Cana of Galilee, a small village northwest of Nazareth,
not far from Capernaum. Capernaum was on the west shore of
the Sea of Galilee. It was regarded as the crossroads of the
Eastern Empire.

Why?
This incident was recorded to show that Christ could meet the
human need and that He had power over the forces of nature.

Wherefore?
Christ is exemplified as being in favor of fine fellowship.
Christ sets forth the fact that the hour of His ministry had now
come.

Content Comments

2:1   THIRD DAY—1:43 is the first, the second day is silent, and on the third day Jesus attended a wedding.

2:1   CANA—Mentioned only here and 21:2 in the NT. Either Kefr Kenna, 3½ miles northwest of Nazareth, or more likely Khirbet Qana, nine miles north of Nazareth.

2:2   HIS DISCIPLES—No longer the disciples of John. They later came to be known as "the Disciples," and then "the Apostles." John maintains historical precision.

2:3   THE WINE GAVE OUT—Wedding festivals commonly lasted a week.

2:3   THE MOTHER OF JESUS—An honorable title for the mother of a famous person. John never mentions her name, and Joseph is named only twice (1:45; 6:42). He may have died prior to the public ministry of Jesus.

2:4   WOMAN—A polite form of address (4:21; 20:13, 15) which in this context indicates a new relationship.

2:4   WHAT DO I HAVE TO DO WITH YOU?—A common phrase meaning either "Don't bother me unjustly" as in Mark 1:24, or as here: "That is your concern, not mine."

2:4   MY HOUR—A reference in this Gospel to Jesus' passion, resurrection, and ascension. Compare 7:6; 7:30; 8:20. Contrast 12:23; 13:1; 17:1.

2:8   HEADWAITER—Originally a slave responsible for the banquet, but here a guest who is on familiar terms with the bridegroom (v. 9).

2:11   SIGN—A special word for John which he uses seventeen times in the first twelve chapters. The only other occurrence indicates the purpose and meaning of the signs: John 20:30, 31. John does not use "power" (*dunamis*) which is the common word in the Synoptic Gospels.

2:11   DISCIPLES BELIEVED—Not everyone understood the meaning of the sign.

JOHN 2:12-22

Who?

1. Jews

They were unable to discern between the carnal and the spiritual. They observed the Passover and sought for a sign.

2. Jesus
   He attended the Jewish Passover at Jerusalem. He
      declared that the temple was His Father's house. He
      manifested righteous indignation. He foretold His
      death and resurrection.
3. Money-changers
4. Disciples
   Their belief was strengthened as they saw Jesus carry out
      the words of Scripture.
5. Mary
6. The brothers of Christ—These were James, Joses, Simon,
   and Judas.

When?
At the time of the Jewish Passover.

What?
The passage includes the account of the cleansing of the
temple of the money-changers. The passage indicates the
coming cross and resurrection.

Where?
Jerusalem, the city built on four hills and surrounded by
valleys except on the north and northwest. The city was
enclosed by walls.

Why?
The passage emphasizes the fact that the temple was a place
for worship and not a place where the leaders should take
advantage of the people.

Wherefore?
The Jews have another means of identifying Jesus as the
Messiah.

Content Comments
2:12 HE WENT DOWN—Cana was in the hills, Capernaum down on
   the shore of Galilee.
2:12 CAPERNAUM—Literally, "hamlet of Nahum." Not
   mentioned in the Old Testament but housed a tax
   collector and centurion in New Testament times.
2:12 MOTHER—The last mention of Mary until the passion
   narrative.
2:12 BROTHERS—The natural meaning is that these were
   younger sons born to Joseph and Mary. There is no
   evidence that they were half brothers born to Joseph by
   an earlier marriage, and there is a separate word (*anepsios*)

which means cousin. These brothers do not believe in Jesus (John 7:5).

2:13   OF THE JEWS—So John typically identifies the festivals; also 6:4; 11:55; 7:2.

2:13   PASSOVER—The first of three named Passovers (6:4; 11:55) indicating that Jesus' ministry was at least two years long. It was one of three festivals requiring attendance at Jerusalem according to Deut. 16:16.

2:14   TEMPLE—This more general word (*hieron*) included the outer court of the Gentiles, where this event occurred.

2:14   OXEN AND SHEEP—Only John mentions the larger animals.

2:14   MONEYCHANGERS—The temple tax of a half shekel (Matt. 17:27) equaled two Roman denarii or an Attic didrachma. But these bore images, so they were changed to the acceptable coinage of Tyre.

2:15   SCOURGE OF CORDS—A whip made of the reeds used for bedding the animals, since no sticks or weapons were allowed in the temple. The word is used only here in the NT.

2:15   (THEM) ALL—The word is masculine, suggesting that Jesus focused his action on the people.

2:16   MY FATHER'S HOUSE—An implicit claim to deity. The common phrase was "the house of God." Note the play on the word "house."

2:19   TEMPLE—This word (*naos*) refers to the holiest place, the very dwelling of God. Jesus thus claims to be the presence of God among the people.

2:20   FORTY-SIX YEARS—The rebuilding was begun in 20-19 B.C., so this is A.D. 28. The entire reconstruction was not completed until A.D. 63. The misunderstanding in this verse is a frequent technique in John: (3:3; 6:41; 11:11; 14:17).

2:21   HE—An emphatic pronoun in contrast with "the Jews" of verse 20.

2:22   WAS RAISED—This may be translated "rose" in keeping with the emphasis of this Gospel. See 10:17, 18.

2:22   WHICH JESUS HAD SPOKEN—John here makes Jesus' words equal to Scripture.

JOHN 2:23-3:21

Who?

1. Jesus

   He did not trust Himself to men.

   He was a teacher sent from God. He was to be lifted up

from among men. He came to save and not to judge.

2. Nicodemus
   He was a member of the Sanhedrin.
   He was the delegate of the Sanhedrin to contact Jesus.

3. God
   He, the heavenly Father of Christ, sent His Son into the world to save the world.

4. Moses
   This was an incidental reference to his lifting the brass serpent into the air.

5. Spirit
   He is like the wind. Life in the Spirit differs from the life of the flesh.

What?
The discussion of the New Birth.

Where?
The Passover was held at Jerusalem. The wilderness was that of the Sinaitic Peninsula.

When?
During Christ's early Judean ministry. It was the time of the Passover.

Why?
The Sanhedrin was excited after Christ's experience at the temple, so they sent an envoy to question Him.

Wherefore?
Nicodemus was later converted. Belief is identified and described.

Content Comments
2:23 BEHOLDING—Or because they beheld. This verb is used twenty-three times by John, often indicating perceptive insight.

2:24 BUT JESUS, ON HIS PART—This is an emphatic contrast with the many of verse 23.

2:24 WAS NOT ENTRUSTING—This play on words uses the same Greek verb as "believed" in verse 23. This phrase and "for He knew" indicate a perpetual attitude of Jesus.

2:24 HE KNEW—John regularly emphasized the special knowledge of Jesus (5:6, 42; 6:15).

3:1 NOW—This continues the paragraph of verses 23-25.

3:1 A MAN OF THE PHARISEES—An unusual phrase, literally "a

human of the Pharisees." This chapter is to be read in
the context of the preceding verses.

3:1 NICODEMUS—A Greek name ("conqueror of the people")
not uncommon. He represents a group of Jewish leaders
who hesitantly come to believe in Jesus. Mentioned
only here and 7:5; 19:39 in the NT.

3:1 RULER OF THE JEWS—One of the seventy members of the
Sanhedrin, composed of priests (Sadducees), scribes
(Pharisees), and lay elders.

3:2 BY NIGHT—Both as a convenient time for Nicodemus, and as
a symbol, darkness contrasted with light in the Gospel.

3:2 FROM GOD—This is the phrase that is emphasized.

3:3 BORN—More properly translated "begotten" as of a
father; "born" pertains to a woman as in verse 4.

3:3 HE CANNOT—Jesus used the word of Nicodemus (no one
can) from verse 2.

3:3 KINGDOM OF GOD—Common in the Synoptics, this
phrase occurs only here in John.

3:4 AGAIN—Since Nicodemus misunderstood this word
with two meanings (again/from above) Jesus is able to
explain the begetting from above.

3:5 OF WATER AND SPIRIT—The one preposition without articles
combines the two as one. Water speaks of purification
(baptism of John to Nicodemus, of the Apostles to the
readers) and the Spirit gives life.

3:5 ENTER—A synonym for "see" in verse 3. John liked small
variation like this.

3:6 FLESH—Not sinfulness but the weakness of the physical
creature, in contrast to the Divine Spirit.

3:7 YOU . . . YOU—I said to you (Nicodemus), You must all be
born again. Jesus speaks through Nicodemus to a wider
audience.

3:7 MUST—This emphasis on necessity occurs ten times in
John.

3:8 WIND . . . SOUND—Both words have a double meaning:
wind and Spirit; sound and voice.

3:10 YOU ARE THE TEACHER?—Emphasis is given to "you."
Jesus used the Greek form of Nicodemus' greeting (rabbi)
here. The article may indicate a special position, or his
prestige as a teacher.

3:11 WE SPEAK . . . WE KNOW—Jesus again used the words of
Nicodemus from verse 2, indicating his arrogance.

3:11 SPEAK—The Greek word is *laleo*. It orginally meant
"chatter' or "speak." In the Greek Old Testament it was

used of the revealed word through the Prophets, and in Acts for the speaking of the Gospel. In John it frequently is the favored word for Jesus' revelation of the truth from God, occurring some sixty times in the Gospel.

3:12 EARTHLY THINGS—That is what Jesus had already said to him.

3:13 HE WHO DESCENDED—The incarnate Son of God alone has the ability to speak heavenly things.

3:14 BE LIFTED UP—Used four times in reference to Jesus (8:28; 12:32, 34), with the double meaning of crucifixion and ascension.

3:15 ETERNAL LIFE—Literally "life of the age to come." Quality is the essence of this life, and like the age to come, it has no time limit. This is the first of seventeen occurrences of this pair of words.

3:16 LOVED—John used both words for love more than any other NT book: *agapao* thirty-six times, and *phileo* thirteen times. There is no consistent distinction between these two words in this Gospel.

3:16 THE WORLD—Not only Israel (Jer. 31:3; Hos. 11:1; Mal. 1:2).

3:20 DOETH EVIL—This pair of words occurs only here, 5:29, and Titus 2:8.

3:20 HATETH—This strong term is used twelve times in John, which speaks regularly in strong contrasts.

JOHN 3:22-36

Who?

1. Jesus
2. Disciples
3. John
4. John's Disciples
5. A Jew
6. God, the Father

Where?

Two places were mentioned: The land of Judea and Aenon, which is near Salim.

When?

No time was mentioned.

Why?

This passage emphasized the fact that John was not the Messiah.

What?

This section included a discussion between John's disciples and a Jew over purifying.

Wherefore?

John clarified the fact that Jesus is the Messiah.

Content Comments

3:22 LAND OF JUDEA—Only here in the NT. Probably means he went into the country districts from the city.

3:22 BAPTIZING—Only in this Gospel is it reported that the disciples of Jesus baptized. Cf. 4:2.

3:23 AENON NEAR SALIM—The location of both is uncertain.

3:23 MUCH WATER—Literally "many waters," a reference to natural springs.

3:23 COMING . . . BEING BAPTIZED—Verses 22 and 23 indicate a continued parallel ministry of Jesus and John the Baptist. Cf. v. 26.

3:24 THROWN INTO PRISON—This is the only reference to John's arrest in this Gospel.

3:26 RABBI—John also was regarded as a "teacher." In Luke 11:1 he was regarded as a prophet.

3:26 HE—Literally "this one."

3:26 ALL ARE COMING TO HIM—The increasing popularity of Jesus has diminished John's audience. All four Gospels report a total response to Jesus.

3:27 HEAVEN—A way of referring to God respectfully without speaking His name.

3:28 THAT I SAID—The first statement is reported in John 1:20, 23 but the second is not recorded in any of the Gospels.

3:31 FROM ABOVE—The same word as in verse 3. A reference to the heavenly origin of Jesus.

3:31 OF THE EARTH—A reference to John the Baptist. "Earth" here is descriptive and not derogatory.

3:32 WHAT HE HAS SEEN AND HEARD—An indication of the reliability of John's witness.

3:32 NO MAN—A strong statement showing the general unresponsiveness of the world. Verse 33 indicates that some do respond. Compare 3:26.

3:33 SET HIS SEAL—As a personal guarantee.

3:35 FATHER LOVES—Here the verb is *agapao*, but in 5:20 it is *phileo*.

3:36 SEE LIFE—The same as "seeing the kingdom of God" in verse 3.

3:36 WRATH OF GOD—The final judgment of God already abides
upon them.

JOHN 4:1-42

Who?
1. Jesus
2. Pharisees
3. John
4. Woman of Samaria
5. Samaritans
6. Disciples
7. References to Jacob and Joseph

Where?
Jesus left Judea and departed for Galilee. There are references
to Samaria, Sychar, and Jerusalem.

When?
The only time reference is to the sixth hour.

What?
This includes the discussion between Jesus and the woman
of Samaria.

Why?
This passage clarified the importance of Jesus as the interpreter
and satisfier of life.

Wherefore?
This passage set forth the true nature of worship. It was made
clear that Jesus could satisfy a thirsty soul with the water of
life.

Content Comments
4:1 THE PHARISEES—They understood themselves to be the
guardians of orthodoxy. Compare 1:19, 24 and 3:1.
4:1 LORD—Used by the evangelist as a proper title. The
Samaritan woman used this word with increasing
respect in verses 11, 15, and 19. In 6:68 and 20:28 the title
is used with full meaning by the disciples.
4:2 WAS NOT BAPTIZING—Jesus was not a mere imitator of John
the Baptist. This is the last reference to baptism in this
Gospel.
4:3 HE LEFT—This word is unusual here. It means to
abandon.

4:4 HE HAD TO PASS—The short route from Judea to Galilee was through Samaria. But John used the phrase "he must" in reference to the divine necessity.

4:5 SYCHAR—Probably modern Askar near modern Nablus, or ancient Shechem.

4:6 WEARIED FROM HIS JOURNEY—Evidence of incarnation. John seemed to say he was so tired he sat right down: Wells were a common place of meeting: Gen. 24, 29; Exod. 2.

4:6 SIXTH HOUR—About noon; an unusual time for drawing water.

4:7 SAMARITAN—Under Assyria gentiles were brought in during the eighth century B.C. (2 Kings 17). The hostility was increased in the fifth century B.C. (Ezra 4).

4:7 GIVE ME A DRINK—The disciples had taken the leather water bucket with them, as indicated in verse 11.

4:8 BUY FOOD—The disciples could buy certain dry foods from the Samaritans without being defiled. But Jesus by asking for water and using the same utensil would be defiled.

4:10 YOU WOULD HAVE ASKED—"You" is emphatic, in contrast to Jesus who did ask.

4:10 LIVING WATER—Physically a reference to a river or a spring, not a pond or cistern. Jesus uses it as "life giving water" with a deeper meaning like John 7:38.

4:11 DEEP—About 100 feet deep.

4:12 GREATER THAN OUR FATHER—This is irony; she unconsciously states the truth.

4:14 SPRINGING UP—This word is not usually used with water. In Acts 3:8 the lame man "springs up." The same verb is used of the Spirit of God as it falls upon Samson, Saul, and David, in the Greek translation of the OT.

4:17, 18 NO HUSBAND . . . FIVE HUSBANDS—The rabbis regarded two or at most three marriages as the maximum. This woman was markedly immoral.

4:19 PROPHET—A spokesman for God who had special insight. This was the beginning of the woman's response to Jesus.

4:20 THIS MOUNTAIN—The Samaritan text of Deuteronomy 27:4 read "Mt. Gerizim" in contrast to the Judean text which read "Mt. Ebal."

4:22 WE WORSHIP THAT WHICH WE KNOW—This is the strongest statement in all of the Gospels indicating Jesus' identification with his national heritage.

4:23 SPIRIT AND TRUTH—Only one who is born of Spirit (ch. 3) can worship in spirit and sincerity.

4:23 IS COMING AND NOW IS—The Spirit is the gift of the coming age, but is given in the mission of Jesus Christ.

4:26 I (AM) HE—This is the only place in his public ministry that Jesus admitted he was Messiah.

4:29 THIS IS NOT . . . IS IT?—Expects a negative answer, but hopes for a positive one.

4:32 I . . . YOU—These are set in emphatic contrast.

4:34 ACCOMPLISH—The same word as "It is finished" in 19:30.

4:35 BUT I SAY TO YOU—Using a farmer's proverb for patience, Jesus emphasized the urgency of the spiritual harvest.

4:42 SAVIOR OF THE WORLD—Used only here in the Gospels.

JOHN 4:43-54

Who?

1. Jesus
2. Galileans
3. An official
4. A son of the official
5. Servants

When?

There is a reference to the seventh hour.

Where?

Jesus had departed from Judea for Galilee. There are references to Cana in Galilee, Jerusalem, and Capernaum.

What?

The healing of the nobleman's son.

Why?

This showed that Christ had power over disease and distance.

Wherefore?

This included another miracle emphasizing the fact that Jesus could meet human need and that He had unlimited power.

Content Comments

4:44 HAS NO HONOR—Reported in all four Gospels (Mark 6:4; Matt. 13:47; Luke 4:24).

4:45 THEY RECEIVED HIM—John presented the ironic situation of not being received generally, yet being received by some on the basis of his deeds.

4:46 CANA OF GALILEE—John reported a round trip from Cana (2:1) back to Cana.

4:46 ROYAL OFFICIAL—A servant of "King" Herod, such as Chuza in Luke 8:3.

4:48 WONDERS—Used only here in the Gospel of John. This verse indicates the lower quality of faith in verse 45.

4:49 CHILD—A diminutive (my little child) showing affection.

4:50 YOUR SON LIVES—The powerful word *(logos)* of Jesus gives life.

4:51 GOING DOWN—From Cana in the hill country to the shore of the Galilee, about twenty miles distant, so it was farther than he could travel in one afternoon.

4:53 BELIEVED—In verse 50 he believed the statement. Here his belief was absolute.

4:54 A SECOND SIGN—At Cana, that is, since 2:23 indicates other signs performed by Jesus.

JOHN 5:1-18

Who?

1. Jesus
   It is evident that He had foreknowledge. He healed a man who recognized Him as the Christ.

2. The Sick Man
   He went to the temple after being healed.

3. The Jews

4. The Father

Where?

Jerusalem, by the sheep gate.

When?

The sabbath day at the time of the feast.

What?

A man was healed and he later believed. Strife was aroused by Christ's healing on the Sabbath.

Why?

It introduced the conflict between belief and unbelief.

Wherefore?

Strife began to gather against Jesus. The man testified that his healer was Jesus.

Content Comments

5:1 A FEAST—Many suggest Purim or Passover. John did not specify, though the emphasis upon Moses in this chapter might suggest Pentecost when the giving of the Law was celebrated.

5:1 THERE IS—Suggests an eyewitness prior to the destruction of Jerusalem.

5:2 SHEEP (GATE)—"Sheep" is here an adjective with an understood noun. It could be "gate," "pool," or "market." It was in the area northeast of the temple where sheep were brought in for sacrifice.

5:2 BETHESDA—There is uncertainty about the spelling of this name.

5:2 HAVING FIVE PORTICOES—A pool in the shape of a trapezoid. It has been excavated: 165-220 feet wide, 315 feet long, divided by a central partition (the fifth porticoe). Stairways in the corners permitted entrance to the pool.

5:3b, This late explanation of the angel disturbing the water is
   4 not a part of the original Gospel. Perhaps there was an intermittent bubbling of a natural spring. It does explain why the people came.

5:3b MULTITUDE—Indicates that the season was not winter.

5:5 THIRTY-EIGHT YEARS—His case was hopeless after so long. Jesus was aware of this by His special knowledge.

5:8 PALLET—A poor man's mattress.

5:9 IMMEDIATELY—This is emphasized here, with *eutheos* a word used only six times in John, with two variant spellings (*-us, -eos*). The absence of faith in this narrative is unusual.

5:9 SABBATH—This becomes the subject of the whole chapter.

5:11 WELL (HEALTHY)—Five times in this narrative, but only once in the rest of the Gospel.

5:12 THE MAN—Or more precisely, "the human."

5:13 SLIPPED AWAY—Only here in the NT.

5:14 IN THE TEMPLE—Perhaps he had gone there to give thanks.

5:14 SIN NO MORE—Jesus did not blame the illness on sin, but did indicate that sin leads to suffering.

5:15 IT WAS JESUS—Liable to a possible death penalty, the man cleared himself by indicating the name of the person who ordered him to violate the Sabbath.

5:16 WERE PERSECUTING . . . WAS DOING—Even more than reported here. This is the first active hostility in John.

5:17 MY FATHER—A familiarity that was avoided by the Jews. They would either say "our" or add "in heaven."

5:18 EQUAL WITH GOD—To Sabbath-breaking they add the charge of blasphemy.

JOHN 5:19-47

Who?

1. Jesus

   He was one with the Father. He promised eternal life to believers. He condemned the methods of His accusers.

2. Jews

   They sought to kill Jesus. They were rebuked by Jesus.

3. The Father

   He loves and instructs the Son. He raised the dead. He has life within Himself.

4. John

   He bore witness to the truth.

5. Moses—(reference to)

What?

Jesus claimed deity. He made His defense. Jesus had unity with the Father. This told of the shortcomings of the Jews.

Where?

In the Jerusalem temple.

When?

On the same day as the incident at the Pool of Bethesda.

Why?

This showed that Christ was one with the Father. Christ must be honored as God. A prophecy was given of the resurrection. This showed the way of eternal life to the believers.

Wherefore?

They overlooked the main details and stressed the minor things of the teaching by Jesus. Jesus asserted that He had a different relationship with the Father than any other person. There were claims of deity substantiated by John's witness, the Scriptures, the Father, and Jesus Himself.

Content Comments

5:19 ANSWERED AND WAS SAYING—This gives formality and emphasis to what follows.

5:19 HE SEES—Reference to the preexistence of Jesus, when He observed His Father. The Son is both obedient and divine.

5:20 FATHER LOVES—The verb is *phileo*. It is appropriate here to "family" relationships yet special in that it is divine love. It is used only here of the Father and the Son.

5:20 WORKS—A common word for normal daily work. It includes the miracles and all that Jesus did.

5:20 GREATER WORKS—Specified in verses 21 and 22: life and judgment.

5:21, SO THE SON—The first part of each sentence was acceptable
22 to Jewish thought but the second part was something new.

5:25 NOW IS—The last age has arrived in the appearance of Jesus Christ.

5:26 LIFE—The creative life-giving power (cf. Ps. 36:9).

5:27 SON OF MAN—The absence of articles emphasizes the quality of the Son of Man after the pattern of Daniel 7:14.

5:29 THE GOOD . . . THE EVIL—Not salvation by works, but the works distinguish between mere physical life and spiritual life.

5:31 IF I (ALONE)—The pronoun is emphasized, implying "alone." Deuteronomy 19:15 requires two or three witnesses for validity. Even Jesus' witness to Himself came from His Father; it is not His own.

5:33 HAS BORNE WITNESS—The perfect tense emphasizes the continuing value of John's witness.

5:34 BUT I—In strong contrast with "you" in verse 33, Jesus did not accept mere human witness (cf. 2:25).

5:35 REJOICE FOR A WHILE—Their interest in John was a passing enthusiasm.

5:37 NEITHER HEARD . . . NOR SEEN—A possible reference to Exod. 19:9, 11, where the people heard and saw God at Mt. Sinai.

5:39 YOU THINK YOU HAVE—The practice of the Law was said to give life in the present age and in the age to come.

5:39 BEAR WITNESS—Present tense emphasizing continuous witness.

5:40 UNWILLING—A deliberate act of the will, a refusal.

5:42 LOVE OF GOD—That is, they don't really love God.

5:44 GLORY FROM ONE ANOTHER—Great honor was paid to famous rabbis.

5:45 THE ONE WHO ACCUSES YOU—Jesus emphasized the present

witness of Moses which continued against them. See
Deuteronomy 31:19, 26.

JOHN 6:1-21

Who?

1. Jesus

   He crossed the Galilee and went up to a hill to be with His
   disciples. He performed the miracle of the feeding of the
   five thousand. He avoided the crowds lest they
   establish Him as a king. He walked on the sea.

2. Disciples

   Philip and Andrew were with the Lord. They took command
   of the situation and sought to solve it materially. They
   gathered up the fragments which remained. They were
   frightened on the sea at first but were comforted later
   as they saw Jesus approaching.

3. The Multitude

   They followed Jesus because of the wonders they saw Him
   perform. They saw that Jesus was their promised king.

4. Philip

5. The Lad

6. Andrew

What?

Jesus was followed across the sea by the multitude. He
miraculously fed the crowd. While returning to the mainland,
He comforted the disciples by calming the sea.

Where?

On the shore of the Sea of Galilee in Bethsaida.

When?

At Passover time A.D. 29.

Why?

Jesus showed miraculous powers over the forces of nature and
over other physical things.

Wherefore?

The need was supplied. Jesus showed that He watched over
His followers.

Content Comments

6:1   TIBERIAS—Jesus is back in Galilee without explanation.
       This lake was called Chinnereth in OT times and "Sea in

Galilee" until Herod Antipas built the city of Tiberias on its shore in honor of the Emperor Tiberius.

6:3 SAT DOWN—Jesus taught in the same posture as the rabbis.

6:4 PASSOVER—The second mention of this festival, in the spring of the year when the grass was green (v. 10). A significant amount of time had passed since chapter 5.

6:5 WHERE ARE WE TO BUY BREAD—This is similar to the question of Moses in Numbers 11:13. Philip's home (Bethsaida) was in this general area.

6:6 TO TEST—Not a negative sense here; rather "to evaluate" his understanding. The disciples did not expect Jesus to perform miracles!

6:7 TWO HUNDRED DENARII—A denarius was a common laborer's wage for a day of work. This would then be over half of an annual salary.

6:9 LAD—This double diminutive ("little lad") occurs only here in the NT.

6:9 BARLEY LOAVES—Wheat was more common; barley was eaten by the poor.

6:9 FISH—The word suggests a small delicacy which would make the bread more palatable. In the NT the word is used twice in this chapter and three times in chapter 21.

6:12 FILLED—Evidence of the lavish supply, characteristic of God.

6:13 LOAVES—No mention is made of the fish. The later discourse will concentrate on bread.

6:14 THE PROPHET—Either Moses (Deut. 18:15) or Elijah; compare 2 Kings 4:42-44 with this chapter.

6:15 TAKE . . . BY FORCE—This word is used of violence (as here and 10:12, 28, 29), of rescue (Jude 23), or ecstasy (2 Cor. 12:2, 4), of the Spirit (Acts 8:39), and of the rapture (1 Thess. 4:17).

6:17 TO CAPERNAUM—A diagonal crossing from the northeast shore to the northwest shore.

6:19 THREE OR FOUR MILES—Literally twenty-five or thirty stadia. A stadium was about 607 feet. Josephus indicated that the lake was about seven miles wide and twenty-three miles long, at its largest points.

6:19 ON THE SEA—The same Greek phrase is used in 6:16 and 21:1 to mean "at the sea (but on the shore)." The context does not permit that translation here.

6:20 IT IS I—This "I am" statement may have divine

overtones. It certainly does emphasize the comfort of Jesus' presence.

6:21 THEY WERE WILLING TO—Or better, "they wanted to," an act of will.

6:21 IMMEDIATELY AT THE LAND—A remarkable comment, unexplained!

JOHN 6:22-71

Who?

1. Jesus
   He is the Bread of Life.

2. The Twelve

3. The Multitude
   This was a group from Bethsaida.

4. The Father
   Jesus and the Father are one.

5. The Jews
   They were spiritually ignorant of Christ's mission.

6. Moses
   (Reference to)

What?

The multitude continued to seek Jesus. Jesus gave them a discourse saying that He was the Bread of Life.

Where?

At the synagogue in Capernaum.

When?

The day after the feeding of the five thousand.

Why?

This was presented to further emphasize Christ's mission. This also highlighted the opposition to Christ. It was made evident that one must believe in Christ in order to have eternal life.

Wherefore?

Strong opposition continued to mount against Christ.

Content Comments

6:25 WHEN—More literally, "when-long have you been here?"

6:26 TRULY, TRULY I SAY—This abrupt response is typical in John (cf. 3:3).

6:26 FILLED—With a connotation of "stuffed" or "gorged."

6:27 ENDURES—One of John's favorite words, also translated "abides." In contrast to perishing, this *food* gives life.

6:27 SET HIS SEAL—As authentication and/or approval. If it refers to a particular event it would be the baptism of Jesus. Compare 10:36.

6:28 THE WORKS OF GOD—What God requires of mankind.

6:29 THE WORK . . . BELIEVE—Jesus indicated there is only one work of God. It is continuous belief (present tense) in his Son.

6:29 HE HAS SENT—The pronoun here ("that one") emphasizes God, in contrast to human authorization.

6:31 MANNA—Commonly considered Moses' greatest miracle, to be reenacted by the Messiah when he came. That miracle was the accrediting seal for Moses.

6:31 HE GAVE—In typical exegesis this phrase is reinterpreted for them by Jesus in three stages: (1) "he" is not Moses, but My Father; (2) the tense is not past (gave) but present (gives), and (3) the manna was not the true bread. Jesus is. "Manna" literally means "What's this?"

6:33 THAT WHICH COMES DOWN—This may be a reference to bread (masculine in Greek) or a deliberate double meaning: both the bread and Jesus.

6:34 EVERMORE—Like the manna every morning, but without end.

6:35 I AM THE BREAD—This is the first of the seven *"ego eimi"* statements which have a predicate such as light, door, shepherd. These statements are indicative of his ministry to people who come to him.

6:35 BREAD OF LIFE—That is, "bread that gives life," as well as "live bread."

6:35 COMES . . . BELIEVES—These words mean the same thing, as the parallelism indicates. It is the human side of being "begotten from above," which is the divine side.

6:35 NOT . . . NEVER—These are emphatic statements.

6:36 I SAID TO YOU—On some occasion not recorded in this Gospel.

6:37 ALL THAT . . . ONE WHO—The first is neuter to emphasize the general quality; the second is masculine to emphasize the individual.

6:39 LAST DAY—Only John used this two word phrase in the singular. It is a reference to the day of judgment, and in this verse, of the righteous.

6:40 BEHOLDS—Here with spiritual insight.

6:41 THE JEWS—Now applied to his opponents in Galilee, not Jerusalem as before. This is probably a change of scene from the lake to the synagogue.

6:41 GRUMBLING—The murmur that flows through an angry crowd as in Exodus 16 where the same Greek word is used in the Septuagint.

6:42 THIS—Used in a derogatory sense: "This one whose earthly origin we know so well."

6:44 DRAWS—Used by the rabbis when they brought a convert to the Law of Moses. Jesus insisted that the initiative lies with God, not man. Compare 12:32 and Jeremiah 31:3.

6:51 FLESH—A striking emphasis on the physical aspect of his substitutionary death.

6:54 EATS—This is a different word from verse 53, and suggests "gnawing" or "munching" as in noisy eating.

6:60 DIFFICULT—Literally, "dried hard," that was both extravagant and offensive.

6:64 BETRAY—This is the first of fifteen occurrences in John. It is also translated in two other senses: deliver (18:30) and give up (19:30).

6:67 THE TWELVE—This is the first of only four references to the twelve disciples in this Gospel (verses 70, 71 and 20:24).

6:67 YOU—The pronoun is emphasized meaningfully here, just as in verse 69. "We," "you," and in verse 70 "I," are emphasized for special effect.

6:69 THE HOLY ONE OF GOD—Occurs only here and in Mark 1:24 (Luke 4:34), in the New Testament. Compare Judges 13:7 (Samson), Psalm 106:16 (Aaron), but especially Psalm 71:22, "The Holy One of Israel."

6:70 A DEVIL—Compare 13:2 and 27.

6:71 ISCARIOT—Probably "Man of Kerioth" in Judah. Joshua 15:25. Judas was then the only disciple not from Galilee.

JOHN 7:1-13

Who?

1. The Disciples
   They wondered at the saying of Jesus and many left Him.

2. Jesus' Brothers

3. Jesus
   Jesus knew their minds. He knew the identity of His betrayer. He questioned the disciples as to their

faithfulness to Him. He avoided Judea because the Jews were seeking to kill Him. He went to the Feast of Tabernacles.

4. Simon Peter
He knew that Jesus was Savior.

5. Judas
He was identified as a devil by Jesus.

6. Jews
They sought to kill Jesus.

What?
Some of the Disciples left Jesus. The traitor was prophesied. Jesus and His brethren went to the Feast of Tabernacles.

When?
Just following the discourse on the Bread of Life. It was at the time of the Feast of Tabernacles.

Where?
In Galilee and then later in Judea which is south of Galilee.

Why?
This showed the reaction of the disciples to the teachings of Jesus. It showed that the Jews were seeking to kill Jesus.

Wherefore?
The betrayer was designated. The disciples manifested their faithfulness. The indignation of the Jews reached its peak.

Content Comments
7:1   WAS WALKING—This reflects the extensive ministry of Jesus during the six months between Passover and Tabernacles.

7:1   JUDEA—Only there, it seems, did the Jews (Judeans literally) have enough power to execute Jesus.

7:2   THE FEAST—Tabernacles is called the holiest and greatest festival by Josephus. It was celebrated by living in huts made of branches for seven or eight days in September-October. It commemorated both the wilderness wanderings and celebrated the fall harvest (Exod. 23, Lev. 23, Deut. 16).

7:4   PUBLICLY—His brothers like the Jews expected the Messiah to work marvelous signs in front of all the people.

7:6   MY TIME—Jesus' time had a different purpose (lifting up to the cross and His Father) from their time (observations of the festival).

7:8   I DO NOT GO UP—Either "I won't go up promptly for the
purposes you suggest," or more profoundly, "This is not
the festival of my ascending," that is, upon the cross.

7:12 GRUMBLING—The emphasis of this chapter is upon the
divisions among the people caused by Jesus.

7:13 THE JEWS—Here obviously, as implied otherwise, a
reference to the leaders, since all of the crowds were
Jewish.

JOHN 7:14-36

Who?

1. Jesus

    He was teaching in the temple. His words were given to Him
    by God who sent Him. He made reference to His
    healing on the Sabbath. He said that He was going to a
    place where they could not join Him.

2. Multitude

    This was the group at the Feast of Tabernacles who
    assembled in the temple to worship. They were amazed
    at Jesus' learning. They said that Jesus had a demon.
    Many of the multitude believed upon Jesus.

3. Jews

4. Moses
    (reference)

5. Pharisees

6. Chief Priests

What?

Jesus was speaking at the Feast of Tabernacles. He was trying
to justify His actions to the Jews who were accusing Him of
breaking the ritualistic Law.

Where?

In the temple at Jerusalem.

When?

At the time of the Feast of the Tabernacles. This Feast was
also known as the Feast of Harvest (Lev. 23; Num. 29:12-38;
Deut. 12:13-16).

Why?

This passage continued the emphasis upon the great strife
that was arising between Jesus and the Jews.

Wherefore?
Jesus claimed to be the Son of God, sent from the Father. He declared that He was to be reunited with the Father. A few more individuals believed on Him as the Messiah. More questions were placed in the minds of His questioners.

Content Comments

7:14 BEGAN TO TEACH—This is John's first indication of Jesus teaching publicly in Jerusalem.

7:15 HAVING NEVER BEEN EDUCATED—Having never studied under a rabbi, Jesus' knowledge of the Scriptures amazed them.

7:16 NOT MINE—Jesus was not self-taught.

7:18 TRUE—Of persons, this adjective is applied only to God (3:33, and 8:26) and to Jesus here, in this Gospel.

7:18 UNRIGHTEOUSNESS—The opposite of "true" in this context. In the Greek Old Testament this word is used of a "lie" such as 2 Samuel 14:32.

7:19 GIVE YOU—Jesus distinguished himself from the Jews, even in the way they received (and handled) the law (cf. 8:17; 10:34).

7:20 MULTITUDE—Pilgrims who had come to the city for the festival, unaware of the Jew's efforts against Jesus.

7:20 DEMON—The Gospel of John does not report that Jesus cast out demons. On three occasions, however, He was accused of being possessed: Here, 8:48-52, and 10:20-21.

7:21 ONE DEED—Not *only* one deed, but one deed which particularly offended them: He "broke" the Sabbath by the labor of healing in 5:1-9, six months earlier. See Exodus 31:15.

7:23 ENTIRE MAN—A typical rabbinic argument reasoned from the "lesser to the greater." Thus Jesus reasons from one part of the body to the whole body. The rabbis permitted healing if there was immediate threat to life.

7:24 DO NOT JUDGE—Or better: "Stop judging . . ."

7:25 PEOPLE OF JERUSALEM—Another group of people who lived in the city. They were not the leaders (the Jews) but were aware of the plotting.

7:26 DO NOT REALLY KNOW—"You don't suppose they realize, do you . . . ?" A speculative statement that expected a negative answer.

7:27 NO ONE KNOWS—The Messiah was expected to have a mysterious (supernatural) origin and to make a sudden appearance.

7:28 CRIED—Such shouting was indicated six times in John's Gospel. It heightened the statements of Jesus (7:28, 37; 12:44), of John (1:15) and of the crowds (12:13; 19:12).

7:32 SEIZE—"Capture," or "arrest"; John has eight of the twelve occurrences in the NT. Six refer to repeated efforts to arrest Jesus (7:30, 32, 44; 8:20; 10:39; 11:57. Two refer surprisingly to "arresting" or "capturing" fish (21:3, 10).

7:32 CHIEF PRIESTS—The first of seven references to former, present, and potential high priests.

7:33 A LITTLE WHILE—This theme appears first here, and nine times more in chapters 13—16.

JOHN 7:37-52

Who?

1. Jesus
   He continued to reveal His deity.

2. Multitude
   They were divided in their opinions regarding Jesus.

3. Officers
   They left Jesus alone and thus disobeyed the chief priests. The chief priests and Pharisees said that the multitude was ignorant and spineless and yet they did not take Jesus themselves.

4. David
   (reference)

5. Pharisees

6. Nicodemus
   He interceded for Jesus on a legal basis.

What?

Jesus was in the midst of the feast.

When?

The last day of the feast.

Where?

At the temple. There is a reference to Galilee.

Why?

This was designed to show that Christ was the water of life. His signs of deity were manifested.

Wherefore?
Division and uncertainty were manifested. Jesus avoided His opposition.

Content Comments
7:37 THE LAST DAY—For seven days water was carried from the pool of Siloam to the temple altar in thankfulness or prayer for rain. On the eighth day of the feast no water was carried.

7:38 LIVING WATER—Moving as a river, not a cistern or stagnant pool. Yet here the meaning is spiritual.

7:39 WERE TO RECEIVE—John wrote after the events with an understanding the disciples did not have at the time.

7:40 WORDS . . . PROPHET—A prophet was known more for his message than for the performance of miracles.

7:42 FROM BETHLEHEM—John did not answer this objection because his readers knew that Jesus was not born in Nazareth but in Bethlehem (Mic. 5:2).

7:45 OFFICERS—Temple police who had been sent out four days earlier according to verse 37.

7:45 THE CHIEF PRIESTS AND PHARISEES—These very different groups had been united in their opposition against Jesus! (The use of one Greek article for the two shows grammatically a strong relationship.)

7:46 MAN—This word is emphasized and used in a way to suggest that Jesus is more than "human" (*anthropos*).

7:49 THIS MULTITUDE—Their derogatory attitude toward the uneducated public was used to insult both the temple police and Jesus; only ignorant people follow Him, they said.

7:50 NICODEMUS—The timid man of chapter 3 was still cautious here.

7:51 OUR LAW—Deuteronomy 1:16 insists upon impartial judgment.

JOHN 7:53-8:11

Who?
1. Jesus
   He came from the Mount of Olives and went to the temple.
2. Multitude
   They came to worship.

3. Woman taken in adultery.

Where?
This took place in the temple at Jerusalem which was not far from the Mount of Olives.

When?
This may have taken place during Passion Week.

Why?
This shows Christ's relationship to the Mosaic Law. The forwardness of the scribes and Pharisees was evident as they tried to trick Jesus. The enmity against Jesus kept increasing.

What?
The woman taken in adultery was brought to Jesus. The crowd questioned Him as to whether or not He would uphold the Mosaic Law or go against His own teachings.

Wherefore?
Jesus showed that His Kingdom brought love to sinners rather than the legalistic piety of the Jewish Law. This was the only instance of Christ writing. The scribes and Pharisees were repelled.

Content Comments
8:1   MOUNT OF OLIVES—Not mentioned elsewhere in John, but frequently in Matthew, Mark, and Luke as a favorite place of our Lord.

8:2   HE CAME . . . PEOPLE WERE COMING—This paragraph describes one visit. It indicated that Jesus taught each group of people that gathered around Him, all day long.

8:2   HE SAT DOWN—A position of authority, whether in judgment (John 19:13) or for teaching (cf. Matt. 5:1).

8:3   SCRIBES—Not mentioned elsewhere in John, who regularly referred to "the Jews" and the Pharisees. The scribes were a professional group, skilled in writing and in the interpretation of the Law.

8:3   IN THE MIDST—The position for a judicial examination (cf. Acts 4:7).

8:4   TEACHER—An appropriate address both for the question of law they asked and for the trap they were setting.

8:4   CAUGHT—The perfect tense of the verb emphasized her guilt, which remained.

8:4   ADULTERY—The verb in Greek emphasizes her part in the act in an unusual way.

8:4   THE VERY ACT—The circumstances and requirements for guilt suggest that she was the victim of a deliberate trap. The absence of the man showed a prejudice typical of the first century. This word is used only here in the New Testament.

8:5   SUCH WOMEN—But Leviticus 20:10 and Deuteronomy 22:22 declare that the *man* was to be executed also.

8:5   YOU—An emphatic pronoun. They wanted Jesus to contradict Moses so they might condemn Him.

8:6   TESTING—Here, as most places in the New Testament, this means to test in a way to cause failure.

8:6   WROTE—What he wrote we cannot know. The next verse ("persisted") indicates that Jesus was avoiding their question. Drawing or writing in the dry soil was common.

8:7   WITHOUT SIN—This one Greek word is very general. Yet in the context of adultery the men would no doubt be sensitive to the guilt of lust. This word occurs only here in the New Testament.

8:7   FIRST—The task of the witness. Not even *one* felt guiltless!

8:9   HEARD IT—The power of Jesus' presence and words was here exhibited.

8:9   OLDER ONES—Literally "elders," but here a clear reference to older persons who knew the sorrowful experience of sin.

8:10   WOMAN—A term of respect (cf. 2:4).

8:11   NEITHER DO I—Similarity with 8:15 may in part have caused this paragraph to be inserted into this location.

8:11   SIN NO MORE—Literally "stop sinning any more."

This paragraph does not appear in the oldest manuscripts of John, and appears in five different places in the late manuscripts (after John 7:36; 7:44; 7:53; 21:25; and after Luke 21:38). The content, style, and vocabulary are so different from John that it most likely was not written by him.

Yet the characteristics of the paragraph indicate that it is an authentic event from the life of Christ, which was transmitted separately for hundreds of years before it began to be inserted into the Gospels at various places. Like the quotation of Jesus in Acts 20:35, it is a part of that great amount of material about Jesus Christ which was not included in our brief Gospels (John 21:25).

JOHN 8:12-30

Who?

1. Jesus

   He manifested Himself as the Light of the World. He was one with the Father. His crucifixion was foretold. He was with the Father. He was the only means of salvation.

2. Jews

   They continue to question Christ. Some of them believed on Him.

3. Pharisees

4. God, the Father

When?

This should follow 7:52.

Where?

In the treasury of the temple.

Why?

This continued the conflict between the Jews and Christ. This passage bore testimony to the deity of Christ.

What?

It was one of Christ's discourses in the temple.

Wherefore?

Christ, according to His own testimony, was the Son of God. Jesus was the means of salvation. He foretold the crucifixion.

Content Comments

8:12 THEM—The crowds of chapter 7, in the temple.

8:12 LIGHT OF THE WORLD—At the feast of Tabernacles a great candlestick was ignited, which illumined the court of the women and was visible in Jerusalem.

8:12 WALK IN THE DARKNESS—Occurs in the NT only here, 12:35 and 1 John 1:6 and 2:11. There are parallels in the Dead Sea scrolls.

8:15 ACCORDING TO THE FLESH—Again the contrast between flesh and Spirit as in 3:6 and 6:63. Compare 7:42.

8:15 NOT JUDGING ANYONE—Either "that is not my mission now" or "I do not judge like the Pharisees do."

8:17 YOUR LAW—The very one to which they claimed to submit themselves.

8:17 THE TESTIMONY OF TWO—This would be two persons in addition to the accused (Deut. 19:15). Rabbinic practice accepted the witness of one parent that this was his (her) child.

8:20 THESE WORDS HE SPOKE—This phrase marks the end of a unit which began with the same phrase in verse 12. Notice the same tactic in verse 21 and verse 30: "said . . . saying."

8:20 TREASURY—Adjacent to the court of the women with collection boxes and storage space. The word occurs only here, Luke 21:2; and Mark 12:41, 43.

8:22 KILL HIMSELF—Their misunderstanding emphasized that darkness cannot comprehend the light (1:5).

8:22 WHERE I AM GOING YOU CANNOT COME—Quoted exactly in 13:33.

8:23 ABOVE . . . BELOW—This is an important contrast to John (cf. 3:3).

8:24 I AM (HE)—This is an absolute "I am" statement without a predicate. It implies deity, as in Isa. 4:10. So also in verse 28.

8:25 SAYING TO YOU—This can mean either "What I told you from the beginning," or less likely, "Should I even talk to you?"

8:28 LIFT UP—With John's double meaning, to lift up on a cross in glorification.

JOHN 8:31-59

Who?

1. Jesus
   He taught the Jews that they must abide in Him.

2. Jews
   These were the ones who believed on Him.

3. Abraham
   (reference)

4. God, the Father

5. Devil

When?
After the Feast of Tabernacles.

Where?
In the temple.

What?
Jesus talked with the Jews about His deity.

Why?
This passage showed that Christ was the Savior and one with the Father.

Wherefore?
They sought to kill Jesus. Jesus is the supreme ruler of the world.

Content Comments

8:31 MY WORD—Emphatically, "the word which is mine."

8:32 TRUTH—Occurs seven times in fifteen verses. It refers to the revelation in Jesus Christ as indicated in 1:17 and 14:6.

8:33 NEVER YET BEEN ENSLAVED—Though under political dominance, they assert, their spirits were free. Jesus countered this in the next verse.

8:33 FREE—Only here and verse 36 in this Gospel.

8:35 THE SON DOES REMAIN FOREVER—Here the subject changed to Jesus Himself. This word for "son" was used only of Jesus in this Gospel.

8:40 A MAN—Or better, "someone who."

8:40 ABRAHAM DID NOT—In Genesis 18 he welcomed the divine messengers.

8:41 BORN OF FORNICATION—Forsaking God in the Old Testament was spoken of as adultery or fornication.

8:42 PROCEEDED FORTH—A reference to the incarnation.

8:44 MURDERER—Gen. 4:8; 1 John 3:12-15. Cain was a common example of the work of Satan.

8:44 SPEAKS A LIE—As the serpent in Gen. 3:4, 5.

8:48 SAMARITAN—Either a charge of heresy, or that, like Simon Magus (Acts 8:14-24), Jesus was possessed by spiritual powers.

8:51 SEE DEATH—A Hebraic way of saying "die" just like "taste death" in verse 52.

8:53 GREATER THAN OUR FATHER—Another instance of irony: they spoke the truth without knowing it.

8:56 REJOICED TO SEE—Or better: "rejoiced at the prospect of seeing."

8:57 FIFTY YEARS OLD—This was a safe estimate. Born about 6 B.C., Jesus would not have been even forty years old.

8:58 WAS BORN . . . I AM—Abraham was brought into existence, Jesus Christ always *was*. This was another absolute use of "I AM."

8:59 STONES—The Jewish method of execution, especially extreme sins such as blasphemy.

JOHN 9:1-41

Who?

1. The man born blind
   He told and retold his miraculous healing (11-25). He affirmed his belief in God (30-34). He was found by Jesus and was led to believe in Him (35-38).

2. Jesus
   He found and healed the blind man. He gave spiritual and physical light.

3. Disciples
   They went back to the traditional reason for infirmities of the flesh.

4. Neighbors
   They took him to the Pharisees.

5. His parents
   They refused to answer for themselves.

6. God and Moses were mentioned.

Where?

At Jerusalem. The Pool of Siloam was southeast of there.

What?

Jesus healed a man who had been blind from birth. This incident took place on the sabbath. This healing points to the deity of Christ.

When?

After the Feast of Tabernacles. This was prior to the Feast of Dedication. It was the Sabbath day.

Why?

This healing showed the works of God.

Wherefore?

The man born blind and his parents believed in Christ. Hostility against Christ rose again. Jesus had healed again on the Sabbath.

Content Comments

9:1   FROM BIRTH—Occurs only here in the NT. The more common expression was "from the mother's womb," as in Matt. 19:12.

9:2   DISCIPLES—They were last mentioned in chapter 6.

9:3   WHO SINNED—Even a child, it was commonly thought, could sin in its mother's womb.

9:5   LIGHT OF THE WORLD—A similar idea was expressed in Isa. 49:6.

9:6   HE SPAT—Only John and Mark (7:33; 8:23) reported that Jesus used spittle in healing.

9:7   POOL—Significant both because of its name and because it was the source of waters for this festival of Tabernacles.

9:9   I'M THE ONE—Here is a simple use of "I am."

9:14 MADE THE CLAY—Spitting, kneading, and applying the clay would be interpreted as work and thus a violation of the sabbath.

9:16 NOT FROM GOD—A person who draws people away from God must be stoned according to Deut. 13:1-5.

9:16 SINNER—Occurs forty-three times in the NT, but only 9:16, 24, 25, and 31 in John.

9:16 DIVISION—The source of our word "schism." Jesus always divides people. This theme is prominent in these chapters.

9:18 DID NOT BELIEVE—The signs did not persuade those who were unwilling to believe.

9:17 HE IS A PROPHET—The blind man gradually came to full belief in Jesus as the Son of Man, vv. 35, 38.

9:22 BE PUT OUT OF THE SYNAGOGUE—This two word phrase in Greek occurs only here, 12:42, and 16:2.

9:24 GIVE GLORY TO GOD—An oath to be taken before giving testimony at a trial; that is: "Give glory to God by telling the truth."

9:31 GOD-FEARING—This Greek work (*theosebes*) occurs only here in the NT.

9:34 BORN ENTIRELY IN SINS—They condemned him for being born blind, because of his sinfulness.

9:37 SEEN HIM—Not only did he gain physical sight but spiritual sight as well. The Pharisees on the basis of their claim to sight were pronounced sinners!

JOHN 10:1-21

Who?

1. Jesus

   He is the Door of the Sheep.

   He is the Good Shepherd.

2. The Father

3. Jews

4. Thieves and robbers

5. Hireling

6. Sheep

7. Stranger

When?
During the winter of A.D. 29 between the two feasts.

Where?
In the temple of Jerusalem.

What?
This was the discourse about the Good Shepherd.

Why?
This was given to show that Jesus cares for His own.

Wherefore?
The Shepherd has power over His own life.
The sheep find freedom, satisfaction and life through the Shepherd.
The Shepherd loves His sheep even to the point of giving His life for them.

Content Comments

10:1   TRULY, TRULY—Never used in John to begin a new section, but only a new stage in Jesus' comments.

10:1   YOU—The Pharisees to whom he was speaking in vv. 40, 41. This was a continued narrative, as v. 21 indicates.

10:1   FOLD OF THE SHEEP—A wall constructed with either open top or branches for partial covering.

10:6   FIGURE OF SPEECH—This is not the same word as "parable" in the other Gospels. It represents a Hebrew word of very general meaning.

10:8   ALL WHO CAME BEFORE ME—That is, "those who arrived at the sheepfold earlier than I did." This seems a clear reference to the Jewish leaders, and perhaps also to political revolutionaries.

10:11 LAYS DOWN HIS LIFE—A human shepherd would only risk his life. But the death of the Good Shepherd will give life to his sheep!

10:16 OTHER SHEEP—Outside of Judaism that is, since God loved the *world.*

JOHN 10:22-42

Who?

1. Jesus
   He declared Himself to be the Son of God by the works
   He had done. He continued the theme of the sheepfold.
   He declared that He was one with the Father.

2. John
   His testimony about Christ is vouched for by the
   multitude.

3. The Father
   He is greater than Jesus. He is responsible for the works of
   Jesus.

4. Jews
   They questioned Jesus and then proceeded to stone Him
   because He said that He was the Son of God.

What?

This seemed to be an informal discussion on the Feast Day. Jesus
proclaimed unity with the Father and insisted that He was
the Son of God.

Where?

This took place in Jerusalem.

When?

In the winter at the Feast of Dedication.

Why?

This showed the deity of Christ. It emphasized the validity of
John's testimony. Here was another instance of belief.

Wherefore?

Christ is shown to be the Son of God because of the works
which the Father had accomplished through Him. Jesus once
more turned away from the mob and sought quietude.

Content Comments

10:22 DEDICATION—Celebration of the rededication of the
      temple by Judas Maccabeus in 165 B.C. after its desecration
      by Antiochus Epiphanes in 168 B.C. Commonly called
      Hanukkah. Mentioned only here in the NT.

10:23 WINTER—The 25th of Chislev, equivalent to our
      December.

10:23 PORTICO OF SOLOMON—Herod's magnificent construction added porches (colonnades) to all four sides of the temple courts. Solomon's portico was on the east side.

10:24 WERE SAYING—That is, kept asking persistently.

10:24 KEEP US IN SUSPENSE—Literally: "take away our breath." This phrase might have double meaning.

10:24 PLAINLY—Or boldly. When they accused him of timidity, he spoke boldly and they accused him of blasphemy (v. 33).

10:26 MY SHEEP—Though Tabernacles (7:2) and Dedication (10:22) are two months apart, John treated the whole period as a continued controversy.

10:33 MAN . . . GOD—The incarnation is incomprehensible to them (cf. John 1:1 and 1:14).

10:34 YOU ARE GODS—Ps. 82:6 calls the judges of Israel "gods" as an indication of the high office given to them by God.

10:35 CANNOT BE BROKEN—Or "cannot lose its force." It is the opposite of "fulfill." The same idea is expressed in 7:23.

10:36 WHOM THE FATHER SANCTIFIED—At the feast of Dedication Jesus declared that He had been "dedicated" (sanctified) by God, not by man.

10:40 BEYOND JORDAN—This reference to the very words of 1:28 indicates that the public ministry of Jesus, begun thereafter, was now completed.

JOHN 11:1-53

Who?

1. Jesus
   He is the resurrection and the life.

2. Lazarus

3. Martha

4. Jews

5. Mary

6. Disciples

7. Thomas

8. Pharisees

9. Chief priests

10. Caiaphas
    the high priest

11. God, the Father
    (reference)
12. Romans
    (reference)

When?
No time was indicated.

Where?
At Bethany which was two miles from Jerusalem.

Why?
Showed that Jesus had power over death.

What?
Lazarus was raised from the dead. Antagonism arose against Jesus which was to culminate in His being put to death.

Wherefore?
Jesus declared Himself to be "the Resurrection and the life." Many of the Jews believed on Jesus. The chief priests and Pharisees realized that they would have to deal with Jesus in some way.

Content Comments

11:1   LAZARUS—A shortened form of Eleazar meaning "God helps."

11:1   BETHANY—"House of Affliction." It served as Jesus' home when he visited Jerusalem (Mark 11:11; 14:3). This is not the same as Bethany beyond Jordan of 1:28.

11:2   WHO ANOINTED—This was not reported until the next chapter, but to John and his readers it was already in the past tense.

11:3   LOVE—The Greek word is *phileo,* but this is not a weak verb in John: see 5:20; 16:27; 20:2.

11:4   SON OF GOD—Only here and in 5:25 did Jesus use this title of himself.

11:5   LOVED—Here the verb is *agapao.* Both words describe the love of Jesus for Lazarus, without significant difference.

11:8   RABBI—This was the last time the disciples call Jesus by this name in John.

11:12 HE WILL RECOVER—Literally, "He will be saved."

11:17 FOUR DAYS—The rabbis believed that after four days the soul departed and there was no hope of revival.

11:20 MARY STILL SAT—Women in mourning sat on the floor in the house (cf. Ezek. 8:14).

11:21 IF YOU HAD BEEN HERE—They believed that Jesus could prevent, but not reverse death (cf. v. 32 and v. 37).

11:24, WILL . . . AM—The tenses are important. Jesus was already
25 the resurrection and eternal life, evidenced by his giving physical life to Lazarus.

11:31 TO WEEP—Literally, "to wail"; compare Mary Magdalene in 20:11, 15.

11:33 DEEPLY MOVED—An intense emotional response, even anger. Perhaps an expression of the indignation of Jesus against death and its effect.

11:38 CAVE AND A STONE—A horizontal opening, with a stone to keep animals out.

11:39 THERE WILL BE A STENCH—With no embalming, the spices gave only brief protection from the odors.

11:41 RAISED HIS EYES—A common Jewish posture for prayer.

11:43 CRIED OUT—A very loud shout. When Jesus shouted He gave life to Lazarus; when the crowd shouted (18:40; 19:6, 15) they brought death to Jesus.

11:44 WRAPPINGS—Strips of cloth wound around the body. Perhaps the arms and legs were wrapped individually.

11:45 BEHELD—The Greek word often suggests spiritual perception.

11:47 CONVENED—The same word as v. 52 "gather together" but with opposite purposes.

11:47 COUNCIL—Literally "Sanhedrin." The word occurs only here in John's Gospel. This seems to be an informal meeting, since the article is not used with the noun and Caiaphas is not presiding.

11:47 MANY SIGNS—Only two have been reported in chapters 9 and 11. Though they admit the signs, the leaders will not believe on Jesus.

11:49 HIGH PRIEST THAT YEAR—"That fateful year." Caiaphas was high priest from A.D. 18-36. Though it was a lifetime position, it was actually controlled by the Romans. The deposed high priest, Annas, was still powerful (John 18:13).

11:49 YOU KNOW NOTHING AT ALL—Sadducees were known for their rude behavior.

11:50 FOR YOU—The privileged position of the priestly class was being threatened.

11:51 PROPHESIED—Prophecy was often associated with the high priest (Num. 27:21; 2 Sam. 15:27).

11:51 CHILDREN . . . SCATTERED ABROAD—In this Gospel a reference to gentiles who would believe in Jesus.

JOHN 11:54—12:11

Who?
1. Jews
2. Mary
3. Martha
4. Pharisees
5. Chief priests
6. Jesus
7. Disciples
8. Lazarus
9. Judas Iscariot

Where?
At Ephraim. The second part took place at Bethany.

When?
About six days before the Passover.

What?
Plans were instituted whereby they could arrest Jesus. Mary anointed the feet of Jesus. Judas deplored the expenditure of money for the ointment. Jews suggested that Lazarus be put to death.

Why?
This pointed out the popularity of Jesus and also the pressure which surrounded Him.

Wherefore?
They made clear their plan to kill Lazarus and also to arrest Jesus.

Content Comments
11:55 PASSOVER—The third mentioned in this Gospel. Jesus spent the first in Jerusalem (2:13), and the second in Galilee (6:4).
11:55 MANY—Perhaps 75,000 pilgrims and 25,000 Jerusalemites.
11:55 PURIFY THEMSELVES—Could require as long as a week if defiled by contact with corpses.
11:57 COMMANDMENT—Every other time in the Gospel this word is used of God or Jesus.
12:1 SIX DAYS BEFORE—Saturday, the Sabbath.
12:3 FEET . . . HAIR—A combination of humility and personal

involvement. A woman would not loosen her hair in public.

12:8   THE POOR . . . ME—Some deeds of mercy (burial) were considered more perfect than other deeds of mercy (almsgiving).

JOHN 12:12-50

Who?
1. Multitude
2. Jesus
   King of Israel and Son of Man
3. Disciples
4. Pharisees
5. Greeks
6. Philip
7. Andrew
8. God, the Father
9. Isaiah
   (reference)
10. Prince of this world

What?
This is the account of the Triumphal Entry. Christ climaxed His claims of deity.

Where?
Jesus was coming to Jerusalem.

When?
The beginning of Passion Week.

Why?
This was the climaxing attempt to save men.

Wherefore?
The rulers of the Jews secretly believed. The Pharisees were still self-righteous. Christ was acclaimed by the multitude but for the wrong motive.

Content Comments
12:12   THE NEXT DAY—Sunday (cf. v. 1). "Palm Sunday" comes from this Gospel.
12:12   THE GREAT MULTITUDE—Festival pilgrims from the country.

12:13 TO MEET—The official welcome of a dignitary.

12:13 BRANCHES—Occurs only here in the NT. Palm branches were symbolic of triumph.

12:13 HOSANNA—Here a cry of praise, though it could also be a prayer or greeting.

12:13 HE WHO COMES IN THE NAME OF THE LORD—Very appropriate to this Gospel which emphasized the coming of the Son and the "I am" statements.

12:15 DONKEY'S COLT—Not on a war horse, nor walking in front of an army.

12:16 NOT UNDERSTAND—That is, the real nature of his kingship.

12:18 THE MULTITUDE—A third crowd (cf. v. 12 and v. 17) which came out of the city to meet the procession.

12:19 THE WORLD—An exaggeration that was later to become accurate in world evangelism.

12:20 GREEKS—These gentiles symbolize the climax of Jesus' ministry to the world and the rejection by Judaism.

12:24 DIES—The important word in this sentence.

12:25 LOVES . . . HATES—This strong contrast is typical of Semitic speech.

12:25 LOSES . . . KEEP—Or more literally: "destroys . . . preserves."

12:32 AND I—Stated emphatically.

12:32 ALL MEN—That is, not only the descendants of Abraham.

12:35 NOT OVERTAKE—The same phrase as in 1:5.

12:36 SONS OF LIGHT—To have the quality of light.

12:38 MIGHT BE FULFILLED—This phrase occurs also in 13:18; 15:25; 17:12; and 19:24, 36.

12:42 RULERS BELIEVED—Such as Nicodemus and Joseph of Arimathea.

12:46 I . . . LIGHT—These two words are given special emphasis in this sentence.

12:48 REJECTS—Occurs only here in John.

JOHN 13:1-30

Who?

1. Jesus

2. Judas Iscariot

3. Simon Peter

4. Satan

5. Other disciples

What?
Jesus ministered at the Passover. Jesus pointed out His betrayer. Jesus exhorted the disciples to minister to one another. Jesus pointed out the fact of His union with the Father.

Where?
Jerusalem (John Mark's House)

When?
At the time of the Passover.

Why?
This discussed the ministry of the disciples. The betrayer was identified.

Wherefore?
The disciples still did not understand the plan of Jesus. Judas was identified as the betrayer.

Content Comments

13:1   PASSOVER—A festival which together with Unleavened Bread lasted eight days.

13:4   LAID ASIDE—Symbolic of laying down his life. Compare chapter 10 where the same verb is used.

13:4   GARMENTS—Jesus now wore only the loincloth of a slave.

13:5   BASIN—Water was poured over the feet and caught in the basin. This word occurs only here in the NT.

13:6   SIMON PETER—Probably the last one to be washed (cf. v. 12).

13:6   YOU . . . MY—The pronouns are emphasized in verses 6 and 7.

13:10 BATHE . . . WASH—A person would bathe at home and only his feet would be washed at the home of the host.

13:17 BLESSED—Occurs only twice in John; here and 20:29.

13:18 LIFTED UP HIS HEEL—A sign of contempt, which is even worse after accepting hospitality.

13:19 BEFORE IT COMES TO PASS—Recurs in 14:29 and 16:4 in echo of the prophetic word of the Old Testament (cf. Isa. 48:5).

13:19 I AM HE—Another allusion to deity as in 8:58. "He" does not occur in the Greek text.

13:21 TROUBLED—This is the third reference to the betrayer (cf. v. 10, v. 18).

13:23 BREAST—Used only here and 1:18. John and Judas reclined at the head of the table with Jesus. Five disciples reclined at each side of the table. Peter was probably on the end of the right side.

13:26 MORSEL—Used four times here and nowhere else in the NT. Since bread was available to all, it was probably a piece of meat.

13:27 SATAN ENTERED—Occurs only here in the Gospel and in the vocabulary of demon possession.

13:28 QUICKLY—Perhaps Judas planned a later betrayal.

13:29 GIVE TO THE POOR—A Passover custom.

13:30 NIGHT—Darkness tries to conquer light (cf. 1:5).

JOHN 13:31—14:31

Who?

1. Jesus
2. Disciples
   (little children)
3. Holy Spirit
   The Counselor
4. Simon Peter
5. Thomas
6. Philip
7. Comforter
8. Judas
   (not Iscariot)
9. Satan

What?

The disciples were to practice love. Peter was shown to be impetuous. This was a comforting discourse. There was an expression of lack of understanding on the part of Philip, Thomas and Judas.

Where?

At John Mark's house.

When?

After the Last Supper.

Why?

This provided guidance and comfort to the disciples.

Wherefore?

There was a general misunderstanding.

Content Comments

13:31   SON OF MAN—Used here for the last of twelve times in this Gospel.

13:33   LITTLE CHILDREN—Occurs only here in the Gospels, and seven times in 1 John.

13:34   NEW COMMANDMENT—Occurs ten times in the Gospel, six times in this last discourse. The newness is the example of Jesus' love.

13:34   LOVE . . . LOVED—The love of the disciples was continuous; Jesus loved by His death.

14:1   TROUBLED—This verb is used four times of Jesus (11:33; 12:27; 13:21; 14:27) and once of water (5:7).

14:2   DWELLING PLACES—Literally "abiding place." This noun is related to the verb "abide" which is so frequent in John. Occurs only here and v. 23 in the NT.

14:3   I WILL COME AGAIN—Jesus' return is thus a "second coming," though most NT reference speak of it as his "arrival" (*parousia*).

14:5   THOMAS SAID TO HIM—This was the first of three similar interruptions in this chapter by friends of Jesus.

14:6   THE WAY—This is the important word, explained by "truth" (the genuine revelation of the Father) and "life" (which is spiritual).

14:7   KNOWN . . . FATHER—These two words are emphasized in this sentence.

14:7   FROM NOW ON—The members of the old dispensation did not claim to know God; in Jesus Christ this has changed.

14:8   SHOW US—Philip expected a theophany as Exod. 24:20; 33:17.

14:11   BELIEVE ME THAT—The object of faith is both the person and his teaching.

14:12   GREATER WORKS—Greater in quantity, geography, and conversions, but not in quality.

14:13   IN MY NAME—This phrase is used seven times; only in chapters 14, 15, and 16.

14:16   ANOTHER HELPER—Literally "paraclete." He is the permanent replacement who is just like Jesus. "Paraclete" occurs only five times in the NT: 14:16, 26; 15:26; 16:7; and 1 John 2:1.

14:17   SPIRIT OF TRUTH—That is, the Spirit who communicates truth.

14:17 DOES NOT BEHOLD—The Paraclete has no body, and the world has no spiritual sight.

14:18 ORPHANS—Used only here and James 1:27. A rabbi who died was said to leave his disciples as orphans.

14:18 I WILL COME TO YOU—Verse 19 suggests resurrection appearances.

14:21 WILL DISCLOSE—Judas expected a clear, physical manifestation of the glorious Messiah and considered this a change of plans.

14:25 THESE THINGS I HAVE SPOKEN—This refrain occurs six times in these three chapters.

14:26 ALL THINGS—In contrast to (merely) these things of verse 25, and the partial understanding of the disciples. The same idea is repeated differently in the next phrase.

14:30 HAS NOTHING IN ME—The grip of Satan was sin, and there was no sin in Jesus (8:46).

14:31 I LOVE THE FATHER—This is the twenty-third occurrence of "Father" in this chapter. It is the only direct statement of Jesus' love for the Father in the NT. Elsewhere it is referred to or implied.

JOHN 15:1-27

Who?

1. Jesus

2. Disciples

3. God, the Father

Where?

Outside the temple at Jerusalem.

When?

The Thursday of Passion Week.

What?

Christ was the Vine. God was the Husbandman. Christ gave a commandment to love. The Holy Spirit was promised as a Comforter.

Why?

Christ wanted to give His disciples the needed stamina to keep them steady when He had to leave them. That His joy might be in them.

Wherefore?
The disciples still failed to see all of the implications.

Content Comments

15:1   TRUE VINE—In the Old Testament Israel is the vine (Isa. 5:1-7).

15:1   VINEDRESSER—Both to till the soil and prune the branches.

15:2   PRUNES—Literally "cleanses"; The words change to the spiritual message here, as in verse 6 also.

15:3   WORD—The whole message of Jesus.

15:4   ABIDE—Or remain. Used ten times in verses 4-10.

15:7   MY WORDS ABIDE IN YOU—Jesus and His words are interchangeable as the divine revelation.

15:9   I HAVE LOVED YOU—The aorist tense here refers to His supreme act of love on the cross.

15:12 LOVE ONE ANOTHER—The present tense suggests continuous action.

15:16 I CHOSE YOU—Literally "It was not *you* who chose Me." Normally a rabbi was chosen by his disciples.

15:18 IF THE WORLD HATES—A real supposition; the world does hate.

15:18 HAS HATED—Has come to hate and still does.

15:19 IF YOU WERE OF THE WORLD—An unreal supposition: "you are not."

15:19 I CHOSE YOU OUT OF THE WORLD—There are two ideas here; both election and separation.

15:20 THE WORD THAT I SAID—Reference to 13:16, where the emphasis was upon humility.

15:22 BUT NOW—Better translated "but in reality."

15:23 ME . . . FATHER—The word order emphasizes these two words.

15:24 HAVE SIN—Only John used this phrase in the New Testament. Here and in verses 22; 9:41; 19:11; and in 1 John 1:8.

15:25 IN ORDER THAT THE WORD MAY BE FULFILLED THAT IS WRITTEN IN THEIR LAW—This is the longest quotation formula in the New Testament.

15:25 THEIR LAW—The one which they claimed and professed to obey.

15:27 AND YOU (WILL) BEAR WITNESS—Together with the Spirit. The present tense emphasizes continuous action in the future.

JOHN 16:1-33

Who?

a. Jesus

b. Holy Spirit

c. Disciples

d. God, the Father

Where?
Still in Jerusalem.

When?
No specific time was given.

Why?
This comforted and consoled the disciples.

What?
Jesus foretold His crucifixion and the coming of the Holy Spirit. The ministry of the Holy Spirit was made clear.

Wherefore?
Jesus made clear to His disciples that though He was going to leave them, it would still be well with them. The disciples declared that they were now convinced that He had come from God.

Content Comments

16:1   THESE THINGS I HAVE SPOKEN TO YOU—This phrase occurs six times in this chapter, and in 14:25; 15:11.

16:1   STUMBLING—Occurs here and in John 6:61.

16:2   OUTCASTS FROM THE SYNAGOGUE—This is a single word in Greek, which occurs only here and 9:22; 12:42.

16:6   SORROW—Occurs four times in this chapter (vv. 20, 21, 22) and nowhere else in this Gospel.

16:7   ADVANTAGE—Or "expedient." The same word used by Caiaphas, 11:50; 18:14.

16:9   THEY DO NOT BELIEVE—Present tense indicates continued disbelief.

16:12 BEAR—To carry as a burden.

16:13 BUT WHEN HE—Literally, "that one"; it is masculine referring to a person. So also in verse 14. The (Holy Spirit) is a person (masculine); the *word* ("spirit") is neuter.

16:13 DISCLOSE—Literally "re-announce," "re-proclaim."

16:14 ME—The pronoun is emphatic. The Spirit's work is Christ-centered.

16:17 DISCIPLES SAID—This is the end of the longest uninterrupted discourse by Jesus. It began at 14:23.

16:19 JESUS KNEW—The supernatural power to know the human mind (2:24, 25; 4:17, 18).

16:20 WEEP AND LAMENT—The loud wailing and mourning characteristic at an Eastern death and funeral.

16:21 IN TRAVAIL—Literally "when she gives birth" (Gen. 3:16; 4:1).

16:21 ANGUISH—The same word as "tribulation" in verse 33. Compare Isaiah 26:17-19.

16:27 LOVES . . . LOVED—The Greek word is *phileo*. This is a slight variation of 14:21, 23 where the Greek word *agapao* was used.

16:33 I HAVE OVERCOME—Only here in the Gospel of John. The pronoun is emphasized.

JOHN 17:1-26

Who?

1. God, the Father

2. Jesus

3. Men of the world

4. Disciples

Where?

Near the brook Kidron just across from Gethsemane.

When?

Thursday night of Passion Week.

Why?

This emphasized a triangle consisting of God, the Father, Christ, and the believers. This was designed to strengthen the disciples.

What?

Jesus offered five petitions on behalf of the disciples. The prayer glorified the Son, pleaded for the protection of the disciples, and provided for the future of the believers.

Wherefore?

This passage set forth with clarity the deity of Jesus.

Content Comments

17:1 FATHER—More personal than "Our Father in heaven . . ."

17:1   THE HOUR—Three times it was announced that His hour was "not yet" (2:4; 7:30; 8:20), and this was the third time its arrival was announced (cf. 12:23; 13:1).

17:2   GIVE—Used seventy-six times in this Gospel and seventeen times in this prayer.

17:2   ALL THAT—The neuter emphasizes unity.

17:3   JESUS CHRIST—This title occurs only here and 1:17.

17:4   ON EARTH—In contrast to "with thee" in verse 5.

17:5   AND NOW—Indicates a new intensity following verse 4.

17:5   WORLD—Used eighteen times in this prayer.

17:6   NAME—The name represents the very person of God.

17:7   NOW—"After all this time."

17:10   THINE ARE MINE—This is the most striking of the two statements.

17:11   I AM NO MORE—The vivid use of the present for the future is frequent in this chapter.

17:11   I COME TO THEE—The perspective is the presence of the Father, while 14:2 and 16:5 refer to departure from the world.

17:11   HOLY FATHER—Occurs only here in the New Testament.

17:12   PERISHED . . . PERDITION—A play on the Greek verb and noun: "None was destroyed but the son of destruction."

17:18   ME . . . I . . . THEM—These pronouns are emphasized.

17:20   THOSE WHO BELIEVE—Present tense, realized at the time of the writer, but future at the time of Jesus' speaking.

17:21   MAY BELIEVE—Present tense emphasizes continued belief.

17:23   YOU LOVED THEM—The Christian believers. The Father's love for the world (3:16) was only preparatory for the incarnation.

17:24   I DESIRE—Not a prayer but an expression of His will.

17:24   FOUNDATION OF THE WORLD—Only here in this Gospel, and only nine times in the New Testament.

17:24   RIGHTEOUS FATHER—Only here in the New Testament. Perhaps there is a progression from "Father" verse 1, to "Holy Father" verse 11, to "Righteous Father" here.

JOHN 18:1-27

Who?
1. Jesus
   King of the Jews
2. Judas
3. Soldiers

4. Officers of the priest
5. Simon Peter
6. The high priest's servant
7. The Father
8. Annas
9. Caiaphas
10. Other disciples
11. Maiden

What?
Jesus and His disciples were in Gethsemane. Jesus was betrayed by Judas and brought to trial. Peter denied Christ four times.

Where?
In Gethsemane which is east of Jerusalem at the foot of the Mount of Olives.

When?
Early in the morning on the day of the crucifixion.

Why?
The cross is shown to be inevitable. The opposition was more pronounced. Jesus had to face His difficulties almost alone.

Wherefore?
Peter denied his Lord at a critical time. The hour had come. The betrayal and trial were here.

Content Comments
18:1   KIDRON—Hebrew meaning "dark" only here in the NT. It was a winter flowing brook.
18:1   GARDEN—An olive grove (rather than vegetables or flowers) on the lower slopes of the Mount of Olives (cf. Zech. 14:1).
18:3   COHORT—One-tenth of a legion or 600 Roman soldiers. The Greek word was also used for a "maniple" of 200 men.
18:3   CHIEF PRIESTS—The current and former high priests along with the high priestly families. Only John mentioned the Pharisees in the Passion narrative.
18:3   LANTERNS—Cylinders of ceramic with one side open to insert lamp and allow light to shine out.
18:5,6 I AM—With the style and force of deity (cf. 8:58).
18:9   MIGHT BE FULFILLED—See John 17:12. Here and in 18:32

Jesus' words like the Hebrew Scriptures must be fulfilled (cf. 1:17, 17:8).

18:10 SWORD—Short enough to be concealed. Such a weapon was contrary to the law on Passover.

18:12 COMMANDER—Lit. "commander of a thousand" though often used of a commander of 600 or, as here, of 200 men.

18:13 ANNAS—Heb. *Hananyah*. High priest from A.D. 6-15, followed by his five sons. Known for his greed, wealth, and power. Mentioned in the trial only by John.

18:13 CAIAPHAS—High priest from A.D. 18-36.

18:15 ANOTHER DISCIPLE—Possibly John; otherwise maybe Joseph of Arimathea or Nicodemus.

18:15 COURT—The courtyard of the Palace.

18:17 YOU ARE NOT—The question here and in verse 25 expect a negative answer; verse 26 expects a confession.

18:18 CHARCOAL FIRE—Here and 21:9, used only by John in the NT. The high altitude of Jerusalem made spring nights cold.

18:20 OPENLY—Bold teaching which was neither secret nor subversive. They used stealth and secrecy, but Jesus did not.

18:21 QUESTION THOSE—A confident demand for a formal trial with witnesses.

18:23 JESUS ANSWERED—Only in John did Jesus answer their indignities.

18:25 NOW—A change of scene from the questioning of Jesus to the questioning of Peter.

JOHN 18:28—19:16

Who?

1. Jesus
2. Caiaphas
3. Pilate
4. Jews
5. Barabbas
6. Soldiers
7. Chief priests and officers
8. Reference to Caesar

Where?
Praetorium
The Pavement (Hebrew—Gabbatha)
When?
Passover, the sixth hour.
What?
This passage covers a confrontation involving Pilate, the Jews and Jesus.
Why?
It is this passage which highlights the title "King of the Jews."
Wherefore?
Jesus had been rejected by the Jews. Pilate had refused to protect Him. The cross was just ahead.

Content Comments
18:28   PRAETORIUM—The official residence of Pilate, who was prefect of Judea from A.D. 26-36. This was probably the palace built by Herod the Great on the West hill of Jerusalem, not the fortress Antonia next to the temple.
18:28   BE DEFILED—If defiled, a Jew must defer the celebration of the Passover for a month (Num. 9:6-12).
18:30   EVILDOER—Literally "one doing evil." The word carries political connotations.
18:32   BE FULFILLED—Six times (see 12:38) this word is used of the Old Testament. This is the second time it is used of Jesus' words (see 18:9); it refers to 12:32.
18:33   YOU ARE—The emphasis is upon the word "you." It is unbelievable to Pilate. "You" is also emphasized in verse 34.
18:33   KING OF THE JEWS—A title which was first used by the Maccabean rulers in the First and Second Century B.C.
18:36   MY SERVANTS—This word is used nine times in this Gospel, eight of them in reference to the officers of the Jews (7:32 ff; 18:3 ff; and 19:6). Here Jesus denied having "officers."
18:37   SO—This Greek word (*oukoun*) is used only here in the NT. It returns the conversation to the original question of verse 33. It was Roman custom to put the question three times to a silent defendant.
18:37   YOU SAY—This is most likely a qualified answer; Jesus did not deny, nor did He choose this title.

18:37 HAVE BEEN BORN—This verb is used eighteen times in this Gospel, and only here of Jesus. But it is immediately qualified by the following phrase which indicates preexistence.

18:38 I FIND NO GUILT The triple statement of Jesus' innocence gives emphasis (19:4; 19:6).

18:39 CUSTOM—The only known allusions to a Passover release occur in the Gospels. The word occurs only here and 1 Cor. 11:16 in the NT.

18:39 KING OF THE JEWS—Pilate's meaning here is unclear. It may have been sarcastic; or an appeal to nationalistic sympathies; or an effort to have Messianic expectations repudiated (cf. 19:15).

18:40 BARABBAS—Means "Son of father," and as such is not a personal name. He is described as a (violent) "robber," not a "sneak thief." The same word is used in 10:1 and 10:8.

19:1 SCOURGED—This was the most severe of three Roman forms of bodily punishment. The other two were beating and flogging. Scourging was a normal part of the death sentence (cf. Isa. 50:6).

19:2 CROWN OF THORNS—In mocking contrast to the laurel wreath worn by the emperor.

19:2 PURPLE—This imperial color required a more expensive dye obtained from shellfish.

19:3 THEY BEGAN TO—The use of the imperfect tenses in this verse emphasize the repeated and intense abuse by the soldiers.

19:3 HAIL—This mockery was based upon the "ave Caesar" which was common to Roman soldiers.

19:5 WEARING THE CROWN . . . AND ROBE—John never mentioned their removal. Thus the crucified Jesus is often pictured as still wearing the crown of thorns, though not the purple robe.

19:7 WE HAVE A LAW—Leviticus 24:16 imposed a death sentence for blasphemy (cf. John 10:36).

19:11 HE WHO DELIVERED ME—A general reference to the Jews in verse 18.

19:12 FRIEND OF CAESAR—More than a term of loyalty, this was most likely a formal title granted by Caesar.

19:13 PAVEMENT—Used only here in the New Testament. It refers to the large stone blocks with which an area was paved.

19:14 PREPARATION—John reflected a different calendar than the Synoptic Gospels. By John's calendar Jesus was crucified on the day before the Passover, while in the Synoptic calendar he was crucified on the Passover.

19:14 SIXTH HOUR—At noon the slaughter of the paschal lambs began in the temple courts.

JOHN 19:17-42

Who?

1. Jesus
2. Jews
3. Pilate
4. Mary (mother of Jesus)
5. Mary (wife of Cleopas)
6. Mary Magdalene
7. John, the Apostle
8. Soldiers of the chief priest
9. Two thieves
10. Joseph of Arimathea
11. Nicodemus

What?

This is the account of the crucifixion and contemporary events. The passage deals with both the cross and burial.

When?

Friday, beginning at about nine o'clock. Reference is also made to the Sabbath.

Where?

Outside the Damascus Gate which is north of the city. The events took place on Golgotha's brow and at the tomb.

Why?

This was the fulfilling of Scripture. Redemption was now complete. The Jewish antagonisms were at their peak. This was the climax of redemption.

Wherefore?

Jesus had to bear His cross alone. Jesus showed concern for His mother and for John. Pilate had made his position clear. Jesus was crucified and buried. Some stood by Jesus but others drifted away.

Content Comments

19:17 BEARING HIS CROSS—Actually the cross beam, since the upright, about nine feet high, was permanently fixed.

19:20 HEBREW, LATIN, AND GREEK—Only John reports that it was written in three languages.

19:23 FOUR PARTS—Thus four soldiers were in charge of the crucifixion.

19:25 THE SISTER OF HIS MOTHER—Probably Salome of Mark 15:40, the mother of James and John (Matt. 27:56).

19:26 BEHOLD YOUR SON . . . YOUR MOTHER—This resembles an adoption formula in the ancient world. Compare 1 Sam. 18:21; Ps. 2:7.

19:26,
27 This was the third "word" from the cross.

19:28 I THIRST—The fifth "word" from the cross (Ps. 69:21).

19:29 SOUR WINE—A cheap vinegar wine, drunk by the poor; probably provided for relief of thirst by some kind citizens, perhaps by the women of Jerusalem, by tradition.

19:30 IT IS FINISHED—The sixth word from the cross. He triumphantly declares the completion of the work given for him to do.

19:30 GAVE UP HIS SPIRIT—John 10:17, 18: No one took it from him, he had authority to lay it down and to take it again!

19:32 BROKE THE LEGS—A heavy mallet was used, which itself was designed as an instrument of torture. Here it mercifully hastened death.

19:35 HE WHO HAS SEEN—The only (male) follower of Jesus at the cross was the beloved disciple (v. 26).

19:39 A HUNDRED POUNDS—An unusually large amount, possibly reflective of royal burials. A Roman pound was twelve of our ounces so this was about seventy-five of our pounds.

19:41 GARDEN—Mentioned only by John. This word is used only four times in the NT: here, 18:1; 18:26; and Luke 13:19.

JOHN 20:1-31

Who?

1. Mary Magdalene
2. Simon Peter
3. The other disciple

4. Jesus

5. Two angels

6. God, the Father

7. The disciples

8. Thomas

What?
The empty tomb was found by Mary Magdalene. Jesus appeared to Mary Magdalene. The disciples were told of the Resurrection. Thomas believed after proof. The purpose of the book is given in 20:30, 31.

Where?
At the tomb.

When?
On the first day of the week.

Why?
This made the fact of the resurrection more certain. The purpose for writing the book is delineated.

Wherefore?
The resurrection of Jesus was a certainty.

Content Comments
20:1 MARY MAGDALENE—Appeared only in the Passion of Christ and Luke 8:2. She was from Magdala on the northwest shore of the Sea of Galilee.

20:1 TAKEN AWAY FROM—The huge rolling stone had been lifted out of its rolling groove.

20:2 RUNS . . . COMES—The vivid narrative uses present tenses and descriptive details.

20:5 STOOPING—The entrance was small and low (cf. James 1:25; 1 Peter 1:12).

20:6 LINEN WRAPPINGS LYING—The body was gone but the cloths were left in orderliness.

20:8 BELIEVED—The "other disciple" (John) was the first to believe the resurrection. There were two witnesses to the empty tomb (John 8:17).

20:11 WEEPING—Wailing loudly now because of the disrespect for the dead.

20:12 TWO ANGELS SITTING—Like the two thieves, there was now one angel on each end of the shelf where his body was placed.

20:17 MY BRETHREN—An infrequent word for the disciples (cf. 21:23). His physical brothers did not believe on him (2:12; 7:3, 5).

20:17 MY FATHER . . . YOUR FATHER—Jesus' relationship to the Father was unique.

20:19 PEACE BE UNTO YOU—A usual Hebrew greeting but here more solemn (1 Sam. 25:6) or a formula of revelation (Dan. 10:19).

20:22 BREATHED—This Greek word is used only here in the New Testatment. Compare creative breath (Gen. 2:7) and regenerative breath (Ezek. 37:9).

20:23 FORGIVEN, RETAINED—Literally, "have been released," "have been seized."

20:25 INTO HIS SIDE—Only John reported the wounding of Jesus' side (19:31-37).

20:25 I WILL NOT BELIEVE—The strongest possible denial.

20:26 EIGHT DAYS—The following Sunday. Both Sundays are counted for the eight day week (cf. 1:29, 35, 43; 2:1; and Gen. 1).

20:27 BE NOT UNBELIEVING—Literally, "stop showing unbelief." This was the only use of the adjectives "unbelieving" and "believing" in this Gospel.

20:28 MY LORD AND MY GOD—An ascription of deity to Jesus. It is parallel to John 1:1.

20:29 HAVE BELIEVED—At the time of writing this Gospel, and later.

20:30 IN THE PRESENCE OF—Only here in the Gospel of John. It emphasized the personal witness of the disciples.

20:31 HAVE BEEN WRITTEN—They stand with written permanence (cf. 19:22).

20:31 THAT YOU MAY BELIEVE—Either "come to believe" or, more likely, "persist in believing."

20:31 THE CHRIST—Literally, The Messiah. Unlike Jewish thought, Messiah was also the very Son of God, and had already been revealed.

JOHN 21:1-25

Who?

1. Jesus

2. Disciples

3. Simon Peter

4. Thomas

5. Nathaniel

6. Sons of Zebedee

7. John, the author of the Gospel

Where?
At the Sea of Tiberias.

When?
More than a week after the resurrection.

Why?
This showed beyond a shadow of a doubt the validity of the resurrection.

What?
Christ appeared to His disciples. There was a miraculous draught of fishes. Christ dined with the disciples. A charge was given to Peter. Peter's death was foretold.

Wherefore?
The belief of the disciples was renewed and strengthened. The argument that Jesus was the Son of God had now been climaxed.

Content Comments
21:1   SEA OF TIBERIAS—Also called the Sea of Galilee (6:1) and Lake Gennesaret (Luke 5:1). This is the longest account of a resurrection appearance in Galilee.

21:1   MANIFESTED—This word, used nine times by John, emphasizes the earthly revelation of the heavenly (1:31; 2:11; 17:6).

21:2   SONS OF ZEBEDEE—Occurs only here; James and John are not named in the Gospel of John.

21:2   TWO OTHERS—Possibly Philip and Andrew (1:40; 1:43; 6:7, 8; 12:22).

21:3   I AM GOING FISHING—Literally, "I depart to fish." This may suggest a return to his original occupation.

21:3   THAT NIGHT—Fishing at night was better and the fish were sold fresh in the morning.

21:3   THEY CAUGHT—Literally "they captured." This unusual word for fishing is used six times of efforts to arrest Jesus (7:30; 8:20; 10:39; 11:57).

21:5   CHILDREN—An unusual address, equivalent to "little boys" (cf. 1 John 2:13, 18).

21:7 NAKED—Underclothes, or a loincloth, were inappropriate for personal greetings.

21:15 SON OF JOHN—This more formal identification occurs only here and in 1:42.

21:15 THAN THESE—Either "than this fishing equipment" or "than these men love men."

21:15 LOVE—For emphatic variety John used two words for "love," three words for "sheep," two words for "know" and two words for "tending" sheep.

21:17 GRIEVED—Because Jesus repeated the question three times (13:38).

21:20 THE ONE WHO—John frequently referred to people this way (cf. 6:71; 18:14; 19:39).

21:25 I SUPPOSE—Literally, "I think." Used only here in the Gospel and only twice in the rest of the New Testament.

21:25 THE WORLD—Either the atmosphere of earth or the entire universe.

But that John, last of all, conscious that the outward facts had been set forth in the Gospels, was urged on by his disciples, and divinely moved by the Spirit, composed a spiritual Gospel.

EUSEBIUS PAMPHILI, *The Ecclesiastical History,* bk. 6 ch. 14; citing a manuscript from Clement of Alexandria which is no longer extant. The translation is from the Loeb Classical Library.

Four

SELECTING MATERIAL
FOR DEVOTIONAL INSPIRATION:
USING THE STETHOSCOPE

The material in this section will prove helpful in many different ways. One of the most obvious uses will be the inclusion of the headings and outlines directly in one's study Bible. Such headings and outlines will provide stimulation for thought and guidelines for further development.

Some of the outlines can be developed into devotional talks or sermons. The expositional outline is here but the speaker would have to develop his own application. An expository message includes both exposition and application.

Many of the organized ideas in this section would be useful in constructing an outline of the Gospel of John. Such an outline would be especially practical for use in home Bible studies.

EXPOSITIONAL OUTLINES FOR INSPIRATION

1:1-18
Essential declarations
   1:1
   1:14
   1:18
Elements of tragedy
   1:5 The extinguished light
   1:10 The unrecognized life
   1:11 The unwanted love
Keywords of the Gospel
   Light, Believe, Life, Darkness, Witness, World

Christ is:
   1:1 The Word
   1:4 The Life
   1:7 The Light
   1:18 The Son
God becomes man
   1:1-5   Divine life is revealed
   1:6-13   Divine light is displayed
   1:14-18 Divine love is expressed
The Word
   1:1, 2 Eternal
   1:3   Creative
   1:4   Living
   1:14   Incarnate
1:6, 7
   A Man with a message
   A Man with a master
   A Man with a ministry
1:9-12
   The test
   The tragedy
   The triumph

1:19-51
Components of a testimony or *great discoveries*
   1:36 Declaration
   1:39 Invitation
   1:41 Personal experience
Witness to deity
   1:34 John the Baptist
   1:41 Andrew
   1:49 Nathanael
The sevenfold witness to Christ
   1:27   Superiority
   1:29a Sacrifice
   1:29b Redemption
   1:30   Preexistence
   1:32   Anointing
   1:33   Prerogative
   1:34   Person
A winning witness (1:35-51)
   A convinced man
   A communicating man

A contented man
A new name for a new man (1:35-42)
Life's greatest change (1:42)

2:1-11
Mine hour is not yet come
   2:4
   4:21
   8:20
The hour is come
   12:23
   13:1
   17:1

2:12-22
The compulsion to believe (2:22)
   They had seen the glory
   They had felt the power
   They had heard the Word
The proof of lordship
   2:13-17 By His oversight
   2:18-22 By His foresight
   2:23-25 By His insight

2:23-3:21
Important imperatives
   3:7 "You must be born again"
   3:14 ". . . even so must the Son of Man be lifted up"
   3:30 "He must increase, but I must decrease"
Confronted by Christ
   3:2, 3 Face to face
   3:4-8 Mind to mind
   3:9-21 Heart to heart
The perfect gift (3:16)
   In motive
   In appropriateness
   In lasting value
God's love for the world (3:16)
   The revelation of God's love

3:22-36
Unveiling the glory of Christ
   3:34 Authorized

Authentic
Abounding

4:1-42
Contacting for Christ
　4:4-9　Attracting the heart
　4:10-15 Arresting the mind
　4:16-24 Arousing the conscience
　4:25-30 Assuring the soul
A searching soul
　4:7-15　A thirsty soul
　4:16-19 A sinful soul
　4:20-26 A seeking soul
Qualifications of a soul-winner
　4:4　　A controlled life
　4:7　　A compliant spirit
　4:18　A convicting message
　4:24b A constraining motive
A Seeking Savior
　4:4　　A great compulsion
　4:5-25 A guided conversation
　4:26　A gracious confession
Worship: The lost art (4:23, 24)
Never thirst again (4:1-26)

4:43-54
Different words describe the sick lad
　1. 4:49 The father speaks of him with a term of
　　　　　endearment
　2. 4:50 The Lord and writer, John, call him "son" a term of
　　　　　dignity, "Go . . . your son lives"
　3. 4:51 The servants speak of him as a boy, a term of ordinary
　　　　　familiarity
Dealing with a frantic father

5:1-18
　"Do you want to be healed?"—That was the issue
　The man needed a rebirth in his desires
　Faith expressed in action

5:19-47
　5:24 How to obtain eternal life
　5:28 A text of great assurance

5:24 The personal Word
     The personal relationship
     The personal freedom

6:1-21
A very present help in trouble (6:16-21)
     Jesus watches
     Jesus comes
     Jesus helps

6:22-71
Great assurances
     6:44
     6:46
     6:47
     6:48
     6:51
The Bread of Life (6:35-40)
     Spiritual strength
     Spiritual growth
     Spiritual satisfaction
A Great Savior (6:35-40)
     6:35 He satisfies
     6:39 He keeps
     6:40 He rewards
6:41-45
     The resentment they feel
     The resistance they offer
     The reward they refuse
The crisis of unbelief (6:60-71)

7:1-13
Reactions to Jesus (7:10-13)

7:14-36
     7:17   Willing to do His will
     7:14-24 Righteous judgment
     7:25-31 Is this the Christ?

7:37-52
Reactions to Jesus
     7:40   Superficial applause
     7:41-44 Division
     7:45-49 Open hostility
     7:50-52 Hesitant faith

7:53-8:11
8:1-11 Amazing grace
8:1-11
   The interruption
   The interview
   The inquiry
   The instruction

8:12-30
Solemn announcements (8:21-30)
   About the Jews
   About the Father
   About Himself
Jesus and the Pharisees
   8:14
   8:15
   8:23
The Great Giver
   8:12 Of light
   8:36 Of liberty
   8:51 Of life
Great questions

8:19	8:33	8:48
8:22	8:43	8:53
8:25	8:46	8:57

8:12
   The source of light
   The scope of light
   The service of light

8:31-59
Being a Christian
   8:32   Knowing divine truth
   8:35   Possessing divine sonship
   8:32, 36 Enjoying divine liberty
Statements with replies
   8:31-33
   8:34-39
   8:39-41
   8:42-48
   8:49-53
   8:54-57
   8:58, 59

9:1-41
Are we blind also? (9:40)
It takes all types of people
    9:8-12   Curious neighbors
    9:13-17 Prejudiced Pharisees
    9:18-23 Cowardly parents
    9:24-33 Bullying Pharisees

10:1-21
The Shepherd-Pastor
    10:3, 14   Knows His people
    10:4, 5   Leads His people
    10:9   Feeds His people
    10:10b, 11   Serves His people
    10:11-13, 15a   Guards His people
    10:16   Seeks His people

10:22-42
Identifying God's people (10:27, 28)
    Sensitivity (They hear.)
    Fellowship (God knows them.)
    Obedience (They follow God.)
    Assurance (They know that they shall never perish.)
    Protection (No one is going to snatch them away.)

11:1-53
Jesus wept
    11:35   Because of sorrow
    Luke 19:41 Because of sin
    Heb. 5:7   Because of sympathy?
What love
    11:1-4   Love's interest
    11:5, 6   Love's delay
    11:7-10   Love's courage
    11:11-16 Love's purpose
The necessity for making a decision (11:47, 48)
Does Jesus care? (11:1-47)

11:54–12:11
Which do you love—money or the Master? (12:1-11)
12:9-11
    The object of their curiosity
    The origin of their curiosity
    The outcome of their curiosity

12:12-50
The five-fold revelation and response (12:12-26)
Safety last (12:24)
This is for us (12:26)
   Our day
   Our duty
   Our destiny
12:23-26
   Glory by death, not by domination
   Glory by service, not by selfishness
   Glory by poverty, not by possessions

13:1-30
True Christian service
   13:1, 3, 17 Based upon knowledge
   13:1   Activated by love
   13:5, 6   Marked by humility
   13:17   Expressed in helpfulness
The beatitude of service (13:17)

13:31–14:31
The secret of an untroubled heart (14:1-3)
The legacy of peace (14:27-31)
Four great questions
   13:36a
   14:5
   14:9
   14:22
Great assurances
   14:1-3   14:18-24
   14:4-11   14:25, 26
   14:12-14   14:27
   14:15-17
The mark of a Christian (13:31-35)
14:4-6
   Declaration
   Doubt
   Disclosure
14:27a
   The peace that is positive
   The peace that is personal
   The peace that is permanent

14:27b-29
  The call to courage
  The call to confidence
  The call to calmness
  The call to contentment

15:1-27
A parable of production
A command to love
Marks of discipleship
  15:4
  15:8
  15:12
Maintain right relationships
  15:1-11   To Christ
  15:12-17 To Christians
  15:18-27 To the world
True love
  15:12, 17 Commanded
  15:13   Illustrated
  15:14, 15 Proved

16:1-33
The neglected one (16:1-15)
  Convinces
  Guides
  Glorifies Christ
The convincer (16:7-11)
  16:9   Of sin
  16:10 Of righteousness
  16:11 Of judgment
16:8-11
  The Holy Spirit—exposing sin
  The Holy Spirit—exalting righteousness
  The Holy Spirit—exacting judgment

17:1-26
Seven prayer requests
  17:11 Unity
  17:13 Joy
  17:15 Preservation
  17:19 Sanctification

17:23 Be made perfect
17:24 Be with Christ
17:24 Behold Christ's glory
Prayer and great doctrines

17:6, 11, 12, 26	God
17:8, 18, 21, 24	Humanity of Jesus
17:1, 2, 5, 10, 24	Deity of Jesus
17:4	Work of Jesus
17:11, 14, 15, 19, 20, 21, 23	Church

Jesus in prayer
17:1-26
Matt. 6:9-13
Matt. 11:25, 26
Luke 23:24

18:1-27
Gardens to remember
John 18:1   The garden of testing
Gen. 2:8   The garden of tragedy
John 19:41 The garden of triumph
The vanity of violence (18-10)
18:18b
He was disgusted with himself
He had disgraced the fellowship
He had denied his Lord

18:28–19:16
The gospel according to Barabbas
Crowns of Christ
John 19:2   Crowned with thorns
Heb. 2:9   Crowned with glory and honor
Rev. 19:12 Crowned with many crowns
A Man who failed (19:1-7)
In his home life
In his public life
In his spiritual life
19:1-9
The cruelty of the soldiers
The cowardice of Pilate
The conduct of the crowd
The calm of Jesus

19:17-42
Three crosses (19:18)
The inscription on the cross (19:19-22)

20:1-31
Peace for troubled hearts (20:19-23)
An exciting testimony (20:11-20)
The dismissal of doubt (20:19-28)

21:1-25
The questions of love (21:15-17)
Breakfast by the sea (21:9-14)
Going fishing (21:3)

EXPOSITIONAL OUTLINES FOR PRESENTATION

These devotional expositions provide miniature messages for use in public meetings or in private inspirational periods. An analysis of the messages will reveal a pattern for message construction. That basic speech pattern can be used in the construction and presentation of biblical messages.

When constructing a devotional message, it is wise to formulate what speakers refer to as a proposition or thesis. This proposition will be a simple sentence which summarizes the content and impact of the message.

This proposition will be developed into a message by use of one of four interrogative words: why, how, when, or where. Study the passage which forms the basis for the message to discover which of these four interrogative words best characterizes the content.

The main points of the message will be characterized by a key word. The key word will be a noun in plural form which will answer the interrogative and also characterize the points of the message. Each main point will be undergirded by chapter and verse from the Bible passage. Since the main points should be timeless in nature, no names other than deity will be included. Each main point should be applied to the listener before going to the next point.

The conclusion of the message should provide the listener with a summary and also with a clear objective for the presentation of the message. The conclusion will combine the proposition with purpose.

The last part of the message to be written is the introduction. Until you have outlined the message, there is nothing to introduce. Begin the message where the people live. You should begin a message with the secular and conclude with the spiritual application.

See *Biblical Preaching for Today's World* by Lloyd M. Perry (Moody Press) for a more complete development of a message outline.

Goodness or Greatness/ John 1:34-42; 6:1-14; 12:20-35
The footprints of the great are often worn away by the winds of time. The same is also true of those of lesser magnitude. Even the twelve disciples into whose hand Jesus placed "the dynamic gospel" (Rom. 1:16) have been forgotten by many. Men have a tendency to remember individuals in terms of greatness while God is more interested in their goodness than in their greatness.

Andrew was one of those "stars of the lesser magnitude." His brother Peter was the one who captured the spotlight. God however reserved a place for Andrew in three chapters of John, the best known book in the Bible. God loves the common people. He does not ask that we be great in the sight of the world, but only that we use the time, talent, and treasure which He has given us for the good of others and for His glory. Andrew had three opportunities to serve as a contact man for Christ and took advantage of all three.

He put Jesus in contact with a relative. "He found first his own brother Simon and said to him, 'we have found the Messiah' (which translated means, Christ)" (John 1:41). As soon as Andrew had found Jesus, his first concern was that his brother should come to know Him. This priority was carried out personally by Andrew. He did not rely upon someone else to do it. Although it is always difficult to witness at home, this is the place where he began. The product of this whole enterprise was Peter, who later became the preacher at Pentecost. The proclamation by Andrew was in simple terms "we have found the Messiah."

He put Jesus in contact with the physical provisions available. "One of His disciples, Andrew, Simon Peter's brother, said to Him, 'There is a lad here, who has five barley loaves, and two fish' " (John 6:8). Some probably had their eyes on the lad and some on the lunch but Andrew concentrated his attention upon the Lord. He realized that the Lord could multiply that which was at hand and satisfy the needs. A minute, a mite (Luke 21:2), or a word when given to the Lord can be used for His glory.

He put Christ in contact with those who were seeking the Savior. "These [Greeks] therefore came to Philip, who was from Bethsaida of Galilee, and began to ask him saying, 'Sir, we wish to see Jesus.' Philip came and told Andrew . . ." (John 12:21, 22). The Greeks were steeped in religion and philosophy which emphasized man reaching out toward God. They had heard about Jesus who preached of God reaching down for man. Andrew either could not or at least did not provide a message for them. He did however know where Jesus could be contacted and made sure that they met the Master. It has been said that only 5 percent of those who come to Christ come without a personal invitation. Andrew was alert to do his part.

Christ still needs individuals who will serve as contact personnel. The first place to begin to make contact is with the members of one's own family. Any material available should also be made available to Christ so that He can multiply and use to meet the need and bring glory to God. There are many beyond our families who are desirous of meeting Christ, but do not know where to find Him or how to contact Him. God takes note of all those who take advantage of opportunities such as these. He does not demand greatness but goodness in terms of using for His glory the contact opportunities which are available to us.

The Forsaken Waterpot/ John 4:1-42
We learn much about people by listening to their conversations. You will find it profitable to locate, read, and study the conversations between Jesus and various individuals noted in the Gospels. Several of these are located in the early chapters of John. Some of the best known are those with Nicodemus (John 3), the Samaritan woman (John 4), and the nobleman (John 4). Jesus was interested in individuals and was never too busy to converse with them.

Jesus left Judea in the south and went toward Galilee in the north. It is recorded (4:4) that He had to pass through Samaria to do this. Such a requirement was not necessarily geographical, though Samaria was located between Judea and Galilee. There were other roads which He could have taken. It is all the more unique that He went this way since the Jews normally had no dealings with the Samaritans (4:9).

It was about noon when He came to a city of Samaria called Sychar. Being weary (4:6), He sat down by a well to rest. Soon a lady of Samaria came to draw water from the well and Jesus asked her very simply for a drink of water. At this point began a conversation which ended in a transformation. In the conversation, Jesus asked a favor (4:7), aroused her curiosity (4:10), aroused her sense of comfort (4:14), and challenged her to something better (4:15). In the course of the conversation He attracted the heart (4:4-9), arrested the mind (4:10-15), aroused the conscience (4:16-24), and assured the soul (4:25-30). Jesus became very real to that lady as the conversation progressed. At first He was a Jew (4:9), then One who was greater than Jacob (4:12), then a prophet (4:19), and finally the Messiah (4:29). As a result of that conversation old guides were changed, old prejudices abandoned, and old ambitions put aside. The waterpot which had marked her as a housewife was now laid aside and she became a home missionary to invite the city to come out to meet Jesus.

The conversation had revealed to her a source of possible satisfaction (4:14). Jesus was positive in His approach, saying that He knew where there was a spring which would provide such satisfaction that she would never thirst again. It is tragic never to be thirsty. This is true physically and spiritually. Blessed are the thirsty (Matt. 5:6). If they come to Christ, He will provide satisfaction (Rev. 22:17; Isaiah 55:1). If you crave peace from distraction, purity from pollution, progress in grace, power in prayer, or pardon from sin, you can find satisfaction in Christ.

The conversation had revealed to her the reality of her personal sin (4:16-19). Sin is possibly the saddest word in the Bible. Sin separates and wounds. The woman of Samaria immediately sought to change the subject of discussion by trying to involve Jesus in evaluating places of worship. He refused to be led to such a discussion when the crucial issue was that of the person to receive the worship. We have all sinned (Isa. 53:6). When the life has been soiled, it is greatly reduced in value.

The conversation had revealed to her the fact that she was facing a present Savior (4:26). She had been waiting for the light, and clinging to the promise though the life was soiled.

Jesus said, your Deliverer is here right now. "Behold now is the day of salvation" (2 Cor. 6:2).

When these three great revelations dawned upon her soul, she could no longer be content to be just a housewife. She could no longer contain the good news. She had to share the truth of Christ with others (4:29). She left her waterpot by the well and went to witness in the city. She started as a housewife, but after having a conversation with Christ, she became a home missionary.

If You Are Thirsty/ John 7:37-52

If any man is thirsty, let him come to Me and drink. He who believes in Me, as the Scripture said, "From his innermost being shall flow rivers of living water." [John 7:37, 38]

David Wynbeek wrote a book entitled *The Beloved Yankee.* When I first saw the title, I was intrigued for I thought that it must be about a baseball player. To my surprise, it gave the life story of a young man who lived only thirty years. His name was David Brainerd.

John Wesley, the founder of Methodism, asked his English church conference what could be done to help the low spiritual conditions of England. He then proceeded to answer his own question by suggesting that each preacher read the life of David Brainerd and become followers of him even as he was of Christ.

There were many contrasts between the mature Wesley and the young Brainerd. Wesley had been raised in a large family and lived to be ninety years of age. Brainerd was raised in a Puritan home in Connecticut and was orphaned when only fourteen years old. At twenty-one, he stated that he felt like a man reeling at the edge of the precipice of sin. By age thirty, he had fulfilled God's mission for his life and God called him from his labors. His missionary work with the American Indians had made a new chapter in Christian missions and had provided an enduring source of inspiration for Christian workers.

One portion of Scripture, John 7:37-52, characterized his life and work more than any other. On the occasion of the Feast of Tabernacles, the priest would go to the Pool of Siloam with a golden pitcher, fill it with water, and return with his people to the house of worship. On the last day of the Feast, the eighth day, the priest would go to the pool as on the preceding seven, but on that day he would bring no water. In the temple was a large silver vessel with holes in it into which the water from the golden pitcher was poured each day. But on this eighth day there was no libation to pour into the silver vessel. He walked along with the empty pitcher as he returned to the temple. As the procession headed by the priest came by, Jesus stood and cried with a loud voice, "If any one thirst, let him come to me and drink . . ." .

This cry of the Christ brought applause from some, division to others, hostility to others, and to some faith. As David Brainerd preached on this text time and again and as others have before and after him, the same varied reactions have appeared.

The verse begins with a *condition*, "If any man thirst . . ." Just as it would be tragic never to be thirsty physically, so it is also tragic never to have a real spiritual thirst. Our hunger may be for peace in distraction, pardon for sin, progress in grace, purity from pollution, or power in prayer. The *invitation*, "let him come to me and drink," includes one of God's favorite words, "Come." We can come to Christ for safety, serenity, and satisfaction.

The *prescription* is simple. "Drink." Faith has three constituents: *longing* for satisfaction, *turning* to the Savior, and *receiving* what He offers. The *culmination* presents a promised gratification. "He who believes in Me . . . 'Out of His heart shall flow rivers of living waters.' " We cannot help in satisfying the needs of others until there is an overflow from our own hearts.

"I came to Jesus, and I drank
of that life-giving stream;
My thirst was quenched, my soul revived,
and now I live in Him."

When Blind Eyes See/ John 9:1-41

In a cemetery in Bridgeport, Connecticut, there is a small tombstone with the inscription, "She hath done what she could." This stone marks the resting place of Fanny Crosby. It was in 1820 in the southeast section of New York that Fanny Crosby was born. While still a child she had hot poultices applied to her eyes which, instead of helping them, brought blindness. Although blind from that time on, she used her talents under the guidance of God to give us some of our best loved hymns. Only in eternity will her blinded eyes be permitted to see again. Yet she wrote,

"Oh what a happy soul am I,
although I cannot see,
I am resolved that in this world
contented I will be."

The ninth chapter of John records the account of one born blind but who was permitted to see again as a result of contact with Jesus. It is the account of one of the eight miracles in the Gospel of John which taken together prove that Jesus is the Christ and that He can meet every human need. This account involves a defying of destiny for this one born blind. Up to that time no one so born had been made to see. The works of God were made manifest in this case however and the blinded eyes were made to see. What would you like to have God do for you? How and when does God work?

As we observe this particular case (9:1-6), we observe that God works by grace. He works when there is a need, not when the individual is "worthy" of the work. This man had become part of the landscape. His condition was marked by blindness, helplessness, and fear. The disciples consider him to be one worthy of discussion. The neighbors gave consideration to his begging. The Pharisees overlooked his need and were concerned about other things. Jesus saw a man with a need and bestowed unmerited favor upon him.

The application of the cure (9:6-24) shows us that God works when man obeys. The instructions were for him to go to the Pool of Siloam and wash. This he did and came seeing. We sometimes prefer to seek help our way and not God's way. We are sometimes hesitant to follow His instructions just as they are given in the Scriptures. God works when we obey His words.

The consequences of this incident show us that God works to bring results in personal experience to the glory of God. A testimony resulted which was positive, personal, and public. Following the testimony, there came trials and testings. Jesus knew all about it however and was close by the side of the tested man. He always is there.

When the people saw this miracle, they turned to the Master and asked for an explanation as to why He had exposed them to it. "Are we blind also?" (v. 40). Jesus challenged them to admit their real condition of spiritual blindness in order that He might cause their blinded spiritual eyes to see. Their spiritual pride was keeping them from seeing God really work.

God waits to work. He will bestow unmerited favor when we obey His instructions and are willing to give God the glory.

The Magnetic Cross/ John 12:20-36

And I, if I be lifted up from the earth, will draw all men to Myself [v. 32].

Confusion has surrounded the cross through the years. At least once a year it has prominence in papers and magazines. If so important then, why not more often? It is regarded by many as an object of adoration and by others as a token of friendship. It is often made of gold, silver, platinum, and studded with precious jewels.

When those three crosses were silhouetted against the Judean sky, they were tokens of shame, not adoration. On the left a robber was hanging on a wooden cross. He had cast away his opportunity for freedom, was getting what he deserved, and was dying in despair. On the right a robber was hanging on a wooden cross. He too had cast away his opportunity for freedom, was getting what he deserved, but was dying in faith. The first robber was dying a blasphemer but this one was dying a believer. It was the Christ on the middle cross of wood who became the great divider. He was dying for sin and dying in love. He made the difference between sorrow and singing, ruin and redemption.

This same Jesus made a boast and a promise in John 12:32. His death upon that cross was to serve as a magnet to draw all men unto Himself. What was there about this cross which gave it those magnetic powers?

The cross of Christ was magnetic because of its *majesty.* Many had died upon a cross through the years but this was a different situation. In this case the Son of God was dying on the cross. "For one will hardly die for a righteous man; though perhaps for the good man someone would dare even to die. But God demonstrates His own love toward us, in that while we were yet sinners, Christ died for us" (Rom. 5:7, 8). The Son of God left heaven's music and surroundings and became obedient unto death, even the death of the cross (Phil. 2:5-11).

The cross of Christ was magnetic because of its *mystery.* The carpenter, from a poor family, born in a manger, not a writer of books or winner of battles, died a felon's death and was buried in a borrowed tomb, and yet was able to call legions of angels to his aid had He chosen to do so. Beyond the mystery of His person, there was the mystery of His power. Twelve disciples were challenged by him to conquer the world. The Jews and Romans were putting Him to death, but with a word He caused the dead to live. Is it any wonder that Emerson is reported to have said, "His name is not so much written as it is ploughed into the history of the world."

The cross of Christ was magnetic because of its *manner of mastery.* Why do we love Him and why are we willing to give Him our lives? "We love, because He first loved us" (1 John 4:19). God came down to man, not by force, but by love. Christ gained the mastery of our lives. God sent the flood, famine, the prophets, and the Book, but they did not give heed. "In these last days [He] has spoken to us in His Son" (Heb. 1:2).

Life's Inconsistencies/ John 13:21-30

The little word "if" is the weakest word in our language. We are often heard to say, "If I had only . . ." But the truth is that we didn't, and by now tragic results may have come. Judas may have often thought this way. He had so many opportunities for good but now has become a character on the stage of life. Was he a martyr to a cause? Was he just an actor? Was he to show us what we should avoid? The sun nourishes the flowers but it also causes the weeds to grow. The sun causes the flowers to grow but causes the earth to crust. Judas was close to the Son of Righteousness and was outwardly a disciple, but inwardly he was a veritable devil. Receiving the One God sent to earth (v. 20) became the testing ground and Judas failed the test. If only he had done differently!

There was an evident inconsistency in his *occupational life.* Six days before the Passover he was at the home at Bethany. Martha was serving and during the time, Mary took ointment of pure nard and anointed the feet of Jesus and wiped them with the hair of her head. Judas immediately exclaimed, " 'Why was this ointment not sold for three hundred denarii and given to the poor?' Now he said this, not because he was concerned about the poor, but because he was a thief, and as he had the money box, he used to pilfer what was put into it"

(John 12:5, 6). If it had not been spent, he would have had an opportunity to get it for himself. At heart he was a thief with a deep love for money. He even came to the point where he was willing to sell his Master for thirty pieces of silver. In considering his occupation, we would think that he would be trustworthy but actually this was not the case.

There was also an evident inconsistency in his *social life*. Jesus knew that there were those of His disciples who though they associated with Him still did not believe. He even realized that one of His associates would betray Him (John 6:64). Outward attraction does not mean that there is an inward affection. It seems almost incredible that one who would dip his hand in the dish with Jesus would be the one to betray Him (Matt. 26:23). Unfortunately these inconsistencies still occur.

There was an evident *inconsistency in his spiritual life*. There was an empty room in his life which when left unguarded provided a place where Satan could enter his life (John 13:27). Unless Jesus is Lord of all of the life, He is really not Lord at all. When Satan took control then the steps downward were multiplied and hastened. What a descriptive statement it is: "He went out immediately; and it was night" (13:30). When Judas allowed that close bond of fellowship with Jesus to be broken, night took over. When we break with Jesus we break with the Light of the World.

Do people see in us that which they have a right to expect to find in us? Our Christian profession lays the groundwork for day-by-day expectancies in our occupational, social, and spiritual living. The inconsistencies can only be removed as we yield to the Lordship of Christ. We must let Him be in charge. Failure to do this was the root of the problem which started Judas on the way "to his own place" (Acts 1:23).

There Is No Substitute/ John 16:1-15
These are days when it seems to be popular to have substitutes for the real thing. There are substitutes for sugar, salt, meat, and a multitude of other items. There have also been attempts to substitute within the spiritual realm. Philanthropy, social reform, scholarly pursuits, and philosophical speculation have been substituted for supernatural faith in a living God. As the church has had an increase in physical resources there seems to be a decrease in spiritual power. We are slow at learning that it is not by might nor by power but God's Holy Spirit that spiritual victories are won (Zech. 4:6). "God has not given us

a spirit of timidity, but of power and love and discipline"
(2 Tim. 1:7). There is no substitute for the presence and power
of the Holy Spirit. God the Father plans, Jesus Christ the Son
perfects, but it is the Holy Spirit who executes and reveals.

We need to recognize that the power we seek is not a feeling,
thing, energy, or enthusiasm. The power is a Person. Note
the personal pronouns in verses 7, 8, and 12 through 15. He is
the "Paraclete"—the Comforter, Counselor, and Advocate.
This new name given in John's Gospel sets forth His new
ministry of coming to one's aid. He teaches (14:26), bears
witness (15:26), convicts (16:8), and guides (16:13). Charles
Spurgeon said that he never passed an hour after his
conversion not conscious of the Lord's presence. God keeps
His promise. He will not leave us desolate (orphans) (John
14:18). A. W. Tozer said, "If we would bring back spiritual
powers to our lives, we must think of God more nearly as He
is."

We need to recognize the process whereby the Person of
the Holy Spirit indwells the believer. "And I will ask the Father,
and He will give you another Helper, that He may be with
you forever . . . . Because He abides with you, and will be in
you" (John 14:16, 17). The eighty-eight references to the Holy
Spirit in the Old Testament speak of His coming upon
individuals. This He did to equip them for special service.
This was not always a permanent coming nor was it related to
moral and spiritual character. In the New Testament the Holy
Spirit indwells the believer. The individual is born again through
the ministry of the Holy Spirit (John 3:5) and is sealed by Him
(Eph. 4:30), as a mark of ownership. Although the Holy Spirit
indwells the believer (1 Cor. 6:19), there are times when
through grieving Him (Eph. 4:30) or suppressing Him (1 Thess.
5:19) we weaken His effectiveness. We are then admonished
to be "filled with the Spirit" (Eph. 5:18). As we abandon
ourselves and let Him take control (Rom. 6:13), and as we
continue to abide in Him (1 John 3:24), His power is made
available to us.

We need to recognize the profits which can be ours as we
yield our lives to His control (John 16:7). He will convict the
world of sin, righteousness, and judgment (16:8). He will guide
the believer into all truth (16:13). He will glorify Christ or in
other words display Him to the best advantage (16:14).

In the world we shall have tribulation, but in Christ we can
have peace. The fact of His having overcome the world can bring

assurance to us and the feeling of good cheer can become our possession (16:33). There is no substitute for the presence of the Holy Spirit within the life of the individual.

What Will You Do with Jesus?/ John 18:28-40; Matt. 27:11-28
Have you ever been caught in an embarrassing situation where you had something that you wanted to get rid of but had no place to put it? It is even worse when you want to get rid of someone and have no way to do it. It may be a younger brother who always wants to be where he is not wanted. It may be a nosy neighbor who is always around.

Pilate faced a problem as to how he might free himself from Jesus Christ. Jesus, who had been the hero of Palm Sunday, was now the criminal on Friday of the same week. Five hearings were held before nine o'clock in the morning. Pilate was confronted with the case of Christ. Would he risk his popularity and prestige and allow Christ to go free? Pilate's wife encouraged him to avoid the whole matter (Matt. 27:19). He refused to follow the advice of his wife, however, and proceeded to deal with the situation. When he finally realized that he was getting nowhere but that rather a riot was developing, he took water and washed his hands before the crowd saying that he was innocent of the blood of Christ (Matt. 27:24). All of his attempts to avoid having to make a decision about Christ had failed. Pilate did not realize that he was face to face with the inescapable Christ. Pilate then proceeded to commit Christ to the cross.

Pilate tried unsuccessfully to avoid Christ through indifference. He tried to get the people to take him and judge him themselves (John 18:28-32). When he learned that He belonged to Herod's jurisdiction, he sent Him to Herod to deal with Him (Luke 23:7). Even Herod's declaration that he could find no fault in Christ was not enough to free Pilate from having to make a decision regarding Jesus (John 19:6). Attempted indifference will not free us from having to make a decision regarding our disposition of Jesus Christ.

Pilate tried unsuccessfully to avoid Christ through mockery. Jesus was held, mocked, and beaten (Luke 22:63-65). The soldiers took Him, placed a scarlet robe on His back, laid a crown of thorns on His head, and placed a reed in his hand (Matt. 27:29). The soldiers then fell down before Him and mocked Him. They kept on saying, "Hail, King of Jews." Jesus is taken before the crowd and Pilate pointed to Him saying, "Here is the man." When Jesus said, "Everyone who is of the truth hears my voice," Pilate responded with "What is truth?" The One who said, "I am the Way, the Truth, and the Life" is here mocked and scorned. Mocking the Master will not free one from the responsibility of making a decision regarding Him.

Pilate then tried unsuccessfully to avoid Christ through substitution. After stating that he had found no fault in Christ, Pilate reminded the crowd that it was customary for them to choose a prisoner to be released at the time of the Passover. Would they be willing to accept the freedom of Barabbas and allow Jesus to go free? Instantly they cried out, "Don't let Jesus go free. Give us Barabbas" (John 18:38-40). Not even Pilate could make a substitution for Christ.

In the Apostle's Creed, which is the oldest creed of the Christian Church, Pilate's name is engraved for the ages to come as the one under whom Jesus suffered. We, like Pilate, cannot avoid the inescapable Christ. What will you do with Jesus?

The Cross Words of Calvary/ John 19:23-27; Luke 23:34-38
Was there ever a greater eight-day period? It went from triumph to tragedy to triumph again. It started with singing, turned to sadness, but ended with shouting. It started on Sunday with the triumphal entry and ended on the next Sunday with the open tomb. There has been much confusion through the years regarding the cross which was raised on Calvary that sixth day. Some have marked it for magic. Others have used it as a token of worldly friendship. Some have covered it with jewels to make it an item of beauty. Calvary's true cross was an old rugged cross which marked the place of the death of Jesus Christ for the sins of the world. There has always been a magnetism to that cross. "And I, if I be lifted up from the earth, will draw all men unto Myself" [even as a magnet draws] (John 12:32). What were the crucial words uttered by Christ on Calvary?

There was the word of *intercession.* "But Jesus was saying, 'Father forgive them; for they do not know what they are doing' " (Luke 23:34). Not a curse, not a shriek, but a prayer for His enemies before He died. He kept on saying, "Father, forgive." "Love is patient [longsuffering], love is kind" (1 Cor. 13:4).

There was the word of *compassion.* "And he said to him, 'Truly I say to you, today you will be with Me in paradise' "

(Luke 23:43). Here Christ provides compassion for an enemy. The first thief had cast away his opportunity, was getting what he deserved, was dying in despair as a blasphemer. This second thief had also cast away his opportunity, was getting what he deserved, but was dying in faith as a believer. Christ made the difference. This criminal had a positive creed (Luke 23:41, 42).

There was the word of *consideration*. "When Jesus saw His mother and the disciple whom He loved standing near, He said to His mother, " 'Behold, your Son!' Then He said to the disciple, 'Behold, your mother!' " (John 19:26, 27). In the agony even of death, He remembered to be kind. The crowds were mocking, thieves taunting, priests jeering, the Savior bleeding, but Mary, his mother was suffering in silence. Jesus always remembers.

There was the word of *desolation*. "And about the ninth hour Jesus cried out with a loud voice, saying, 'Eli, Eli lama sabachthani?' that is, 'My God, My God, why hast Thou forsaken Me?' " (Matt. 27:46). No greater anguish has ever been put into a sentence. The sun can not even watch any longer and it becomes as midnight at midday. God forsook His Son as He died for our sins that He would never have to forsake us. "God was in Christ reconciling the world to Himself" (2 Cor. 5:19).

There was the word of *lamentation*. "After this, Jesus, knowing that all things had already been accomplished, in order that the Scripture might be fulfilled, said, 'I am thirsty' " (John 19:28). This was the only cry of pain during the whole time of torture. One can live days without food, but only hours without water.

There was the word of *jubilation*. "When Jesus therefore had received the sour wine, He said, 'It is finished!' And He bowed His head, and gave up His spirit" (John 19:30). This was the worker's cry of achievement and the sufferer's cry of relief. The prophecies were now completed. The sacrificial work had come to fulfillment. The sufferings were now nearly over. *"Tetelestai"* (It is finished).

There was finally the word of *consecration*. "And Jesus, crying out with a loud voice said, 'Father into Thy hands I commit My spirit.' And having said this, He breathed His last" (Luke 23:46). He closed as He started—with a prayer. He deposited His spirit with the Father and filed His report. The great transaction was then complete.

But none of the ransomed ever knew
how deep were the waters crossed,
Nor how dark was the night that the Lord passed through
e'er He found His sheep that was lost.

[from *The Ninety and Nine*]

God Took Care of the Tomb/ John 20:1-18

The first Easter sermon was a shocking one. The sermon had
three points and was preached from a stone pulpit. First of all
was the declaration: "He Is Risen" (Matt. 28:6). Then came the
invitation "Come and See" (Matt. 28:6). The final portion
consisted of an exhortation "Go and Tell" (Matt. 28:7). The
weeping women who went to the tomb to hold a funeral left
in a hurry and announced to the world, "But now Christ has
been raised from the dead" (1 Cor. 15:20). "Death is no
longer master over Him" (Romans 6:9). That Easter experience
turned the little community of disciples upside down. The
formerly dejected disciples became martyrs for the Master.

Easter is either a stupendous fact or a horrible lie. Only
Christianity has an open tomb. This is a peculiar fact. The
resurrection of Christ is also a pivotal fact. Without it our
preaching is vain, we are false witnesses, we are still in our
sins, and there is no hope for our resurrection (1 Cor. 15). It
was a public fact that the world could observe. It was a
purposeful fact in that it set God's stamp of deity upon His
Son. Easter is the anniversary of God's mighty act whereby
Christ became victor.

God supplied a vision (John 20:1). Jesus had already gone.
The stone had been rolled away not to let Christ out but to
allow the watchers of the morning an opportunity to see that
Christ was not there. Rome had laughed at His weakness,
but Rome's power had been broken. Twelve frail disciples were
to shake the world with the dynamic Gospel. It was a vision
of power.

God supplied a verification (John 20:6, 7). Theories have
been propounded by men as excuses whereby they might
escape admitting the fact that Christ rose from the dead. God
provided some facts to prove that Christ did rise. Myrrh glues
linen to the body of the dead no less firmly than lead, and
yet when they came to the tomb, the body was gone, but no
pieces of the covering were strewn around. Jesus had not
hastened away. The handkerchief which had been tenderly laid
over His face in burial was now folded to one side (20:7).

Mary saw the stone rolled away (John 20:1). The word here used for "see" is the natural word meaning "to observe." Peter then came to the tomb and saw the clothes and napkin. Verse 6 says that he looked critically and carefully. John then came and saw the clothes and napkin, and the Scripture uses a different word to delineate his experience. He looked with intelligent comprehension which resulted in belief in that which he had witnessed. These had not seen Christ yet following the resurrection, but they had seen the empty tomb and that was enough to convince them.

God supplied a vitality (John 20:17). In their previous fellowship they had been "clinging to Christ." They were told to cling to Him no longer but rather to go and proclaim that they had seen the Lord. The forgotten mission of Friday is now stabilized on Sunday. They can now truly be ambassadors on behalf of Christ.

God supplied a vision, a verification, and a vitality that Easter might be personal. Because of the empty tomb we have the comfort, assurance, and understanding as we look forward to that last great Easter. He is risen. Come and see. Go and tell.

More Beyond/ John 20:1-18
There is something within us which cries out for that which is beyond our present sphere of reach. We build and plan to reach planets beyond. We set the telescope for the nearest star though it could not be reached in 4½ years if we traveled at the speed of light.

Francis Bacon, the sixteenth-century philosopher, had a special bookmark designed which depicted a small ship sailing through the raised Pillars of Hercules out toward a wide expanse of ocean. On the prow of the little ship he had inscribed the two words "More Beyond." Einstein shifted in the midst of his learning from the field of mathematics to that of physics. He felt that the atom was like an endless ocean and that as one studied it he would soon find himself fingering the fringes of the infinite.

On the Friday Christ was crucified dreams were shattered, hopes were disappointed, and promises apparently left unfulfilled. Then the two Marys went to the tomb three days later. What they saw was the source of the eternal message of hope: "Christ is risen." God had rolled away the stone so mankind could see that Christ was no longer there. Out from this open tomb there came the declaration of truth that there was "more beyond." The great assurances of that first Easter provided man with hope as he faced death, loneliness, and the need for forgiveness of sins.

There came the assurance that death does not have dominion and that death is not sovereign (Rom. 6:9). Aristotle had said, "Death is a dreadful thing for it is the end." Touch the veins of Scripture in the Old or the New Testament and you will feel the pulse-beat of the resurrection. The promises of the prophets are confirmed. "Thy dead shall live . . ." (Isa. 26:19). Whittier in his work "Snowbound" has put the truth in these words: "Alas for him who never sees the stars shine through his cypress trees . . . Who hopeless lays his dead away . . . Who hath not learned in hours of faith that life is ever lord of death."

There came the assurance that the Lord by His presence would care for the loneliness of His followers (John 20:13). It was the risen Christ who gave the Great Commission including the assurance that He would be with His followers even unto the end of the age. Stephen at the time of his martyrdom had only to lift his eyes to see his Lord standing at the right hand of God the Father ready to come to his aid. In the first ten verses of John 20, Christ is the conqueror. In verses 19 and 20, He is the commissioner. In verses 16 and 17, He is the companion. Christ has promised to come again and to receive His own unto Himself that where He is there we may be also (John 14:1-3).

There came the assurance that there was a provision for the forgiveness of sins. "He showed them both His hands and His side" (John 20:20). "But we do see Him who has been made for a little while lower than the angels, namely Jesus, because of the suffering of death crowned with glory and honor, that by the grace of God He might taste death for every one" (Heb. 2:9). He died for our sins and was raised for our justification. There is no such thing as atonement and reconciliation without the resurrection. The resurrection is God's signed document that He is satisfied with the substitute and sacrifice for sins.

There is "more beyond." Peter Marshall could say in truth the night of his passing, "I'll see you in the morning."

Sifted but Spared/ John 21:15-19; Luke 22:31-34
The meaning of the word "saint" is confusing. Some have been designated saints but later their sainthood was denied. Some have been called "saint" by man, but we have

questioned at times whether or not God would so label them. One of the most confusing, controversial, and contradictory saints of all time is Peter, referred to by Lloyd Douglas in his book as *the Big Fisherman*. He had been introduced to Jesus by his brother Andrew (John 1). Jesus looked at him and said, "So you are Simon the son of John? You shall be called Cephas" (Aramaic for stone). From that point the polishing process went on. Peter was not just a simple believer to be classified as an occasional companion of Christ. Peter was one of the saints selected for development as a disciple.

Satan seems to be very interested in testing and trying those whom Jesus sets aside for specialized service. Satan thus desired to sift Peter like wheat, but Christ prayed for him and spared him (Luke 22:31). It is not easy to develop a temptation-proof life. As we survey Peter's experiences as Christ worked with him, it becomes clear that the fisherman had to learn some lessons the hard way.

Peter had to learn that involvement demands investment (Luke 5:1-11). As the disciples changed their occupation from fishing for fish to fishing for men, they left everything and followed Jesus. They later became concerned over this fact and had to be reassured that in the new world, they would be more than adequately reimbursed (Matt. 19:27). In Peter's later ministry for Christ, he did not have silver and gold to give but in the name of Jesus he did have miracle working power which no amount of money could have purchased (Acts 3:6). It is one of the marks of maturity to be willing to sacrifice something now for that which is now unseen but which will be of greater value in the future.

Peter had to learn that presumption can lead to peril (Matt. 26:30-35). Peter could boast that even though it meant dying for Christ, he would not deny Him. Yet in the test he miserably failed (Matt. 26:69-75). A little faith can be dangerous. It was Peter who had enough faith to start out upon the water to meet Christ, but not enough faith to keep looking up and thus stay out of the waves (Matt. 14:22-33).

Peter had to learn that privilege doesn't necessarily mean power (Matt. 17:1-21). He was privileged to be with Christ on the mountain of transfiguration. He had seen the vision, met the visitors, and heard the voice. It was within that same chapter, however, that the parent of the epileptic son brought him to Jesus because the privileged disciples lacked the power to set him free.

Peter had to learn that Christianity is not a code (Matt. 18:21, 22). He had to know that forgiveness cannot be counted out by number. The Christian does not stop forgiving when he reaches the number seven but proceeds toward unlimited forgiveness. Having been forgiven so much ourselves, it behooves us to put no code of limitations upon our forgiveness of others.

Peter had to learn that good intentions cannot take the place of good actions (John 18:10). Peter wanted to protect Christ. This was a good intention, but he proceeded in haste and contrary to the method and purpose of Christ. It is not enough to mean well.

Peter had to learn that teaching from God takes precedence over the traditions of men (Acts 10:9-18). We, like Peter, have a tendency to join the cult of conformity. We hesitate to do that which we have not done before though the call to change comes to us as a message from heaven.

Even with all of his shortcomings, Peter heads all the lists of disciples in the Bible. This spared saint found a blessed place in the service of the Savior (John 21:15-19).

CONCLUSION

We look at the Good News as recorded by John through the telescope and see the broad landscape. Our eyes sparkle. We look through the microscope and see the little things which are so significant to this record. Our minds are intrigued. When we use the stethoscope our hearts are strangely warmed. The fourth Gospel touches the heart of Christ. John leads us past the veil into the holy of holies. Here is the inmost temple, filled with the glory of God. John meditated upon all things which he had seen and heard and put down his conclusions regarding them. In this Gospel, we have a commentary along with a biography.

The central thought of the Gospel of John is the incarnation, the Word which became flesh and dwelt among us. The keynote in the Synoptics is the kingdom of God, but the keynote in the Gospel of John is the Son of God. John has told us all that he cared to say in about thirty pages, but at the same time he said that if all had been written which might have been, the world could not contain all the books covering the theme (21:25). It is a remarkable Gospel because of the material which it omits. It may be the most valued of the Gospels because of the items which it adds to the Synoptics. About 92 percent of the content of the Gospel of John is peculiar to itself.

In Matthew we see the credentials of Christ. In Mark's Gospel we see His power. In Luke's Gospel we see His nature, what He was like. In John's Gospel we see who He really was. He was none other than the Son of God. We are blessed in knowing Him but there is greater blessing through believing in Him.

APPENDICES

A CHART SHOWING THE RELATIONSHIP BETWEEN THE GOSPEL OF JOHN AND THE REMAINDER OF THE NEW TESTAMENT

	Date	Author	Pivotal Verses	Pivotal Words	Possible Themes
	A.D.			Kingdom of heaven Fulfilled	The Gospel of the Kingdom
1. Matt.	65	Matthew	27:37	Son of David	Jesus, the King
2. Mark	59	John Mark	10:45 2:10	Straightway Kingdom of God Immediately Service	Jesus, the Servant
3. Luke	61	Luke	1:14 19:10	Son of Man, Jesus	Jesus, the Man
4. John	90	John	20:30, 31	Life, Believe	Jesus, the Son of God
5. Acts	61	Luke	1:8	Witness Power, Holy Spirit	The development of Christianity under the Holy Spirit
6. Romans	55	Paul	1:16, 17	Salvation Righteousness	Justification by faith: its method and result
7. 1 Cor.	54	Paul	2:7, 8 1:2, 3	Grace, Wisdom	Christian conduct
8. 2 Cor.	55	Paul	7:6, 7 12:9	Comfort, Ministry	The greatest Apostle of the Christian Church

9. Gal.	48	Paul	2:20 3:2; 5:1	Faith, Law, Grace	Christ: The Deliverer from the Law
10. Eph.	60	Paul	1:3; 4:13 3:19	In Christ All, Fullness, Church	The Church: the body of Christ
11. Phil.	61	Paul	4:4; 1:21 3:7, 14	Gain, Rejoice	Rejoice in the Lord
12. Col.	60	Paul	2:10 3:3	Complete Christ, Lord	The preeminent Christ
13. 1 Thess.	51	Paul	1:10 5:16-18	Brethren Christ, Lord	The second coming of the Lord
14. 2 Thess.	51	Paul	3:5	Christ	The second coming of the Lord
15. 1 Tim.	62	Paul	1:15 3:9	Command, Teach Doctrine, Good Works, God- liness	The pastor's charge
16. 2 Tim.	63	Paul	1:13 4:7, 8	Ashamed, Endure	The necessity for straight living
17. Titus	62	Paul	2:10 3:8, 9	Sound, Adorn, Profitable, Sober, Good Works	Encourage belief in the practice of sound doctrine
18. Philem.	60	Paul	9, 17	Receive, Love	Christian Servitude— The practice of Christian forgiveness
19. Heb.	64	Uncertain from evidence	11:40	Better, Son, Covenant	Jesus: High Priest and Mediator of NT
20. James	45	James, brother of Jesus	1:22 2:26	Brethren, Faith Doer, Works, Wisdom	The practice of faith
21. 1 Peter	62	Peter	2:16, 17	Precious, Suffering, Behavior	Victory over Suffering
22. 2 Peter	63	Peter	1:21	Remembrance	Steadfastness until judgment
23. 1 John	90	John	3:1 5:13	Know, Love, Fellowship, Flesh	The divine family; Jesus, the Son of God, the letter of love
24. 2 John	90	John	6	Truth, Walk	The value of doctrine
25. 3 John	90	John	8	Truth, Fellow- helper	Christian hospitality
26. Jude	63	Jude	3, 21, 24, 25	Keep, Kept	Constancy amid corruption
27. Rev.	95	John	1:1 1:19	Revelation, Seven, Lamb	Jesus, the Lamb of God

A CHART SHOWING THE RELATIONSHIP BETWEEN THE GOSPEL OF JOHN AND THE SYNOPTICS

Item	Matthew	Mark	Luke	John
Date	AD 65	59	61	90
Chapters	28	16	24	21
Verses	1,071	666	1,151	879
Period Covered	36 years	4 years	37 years	4 years
Directed to	Jews	Romans	Greeks	World
Christ	King	Servant	Man	Son of God
Emphasis	Sovereignty	Humility	Humanity	Deity
Sign	Lion	Ox	Man	Eagle
Ending	Resurrection	Empty tomb	Promise of the Spirit	Promise of the Second Coming
Place of Writing	Antioch	Rome	Rome	Ephesus
Time to Read	2 hours	1¼ hours	2¼ hours	1½ hours
Key Verse	27:37	10:45	19:10	20:30, 31
Key Word	Kingdom	Service	Salvation	Believe
Purpose	Presentation of Christ			Interpretation of Christ

THE OLD TESTAMENT IN JOHN'S GOSPEL

John's Gospel contains probably no fewer than 124 references to the Old Testament. There are nineteen quotations from six of the Old Testament books. These books are Exodus, Numbers, Deuteronomy, Psalms, Isaiah, and Zechariah. Beyond this there are about 105 allusions to twelve books of the Old Testament.

Seven times reference is made to Scripture's being fulfilled: *8:18, 15:25, 17:12, 18:9* and *19:24, 28, 36.*

MATERIAL PECULIAR TO JOHN

Over 90 percent of the material in the Fourth Gospel is peculiar to it. Of the material peculiar to John's Gospel, note especially the interview with Nicodemus (3:1-21); Jesus in Samaria (4:5-42); healing of the man born blind (Ch. 9); the raising of Lazarus (Ch. 11); the interview with the Greeks (12:20-50); six miracles; the discourses, and the conclusion (Ch. 21).

Mark the following passages in your Bible (preferably in color) and indicate in some way that they show material which is found elsewhere.

Practically all that is not peculiar in this Gospel is:

4:3
6:1-21
12:2-8, 12-19
8:21, 22, 36-38
18:1, 3, 10, 11, 25-28a, 33, 38b-40
19:16-23a, 28-30, 38, 40-42
20:1-3, 19b-20

The Evangelist attempted to arrange much of the material in historical sequence. He distinguished five distinct days on which something happened (i. 28, 29, 35, 39, 43); and other such notes of time are:

"The third day" (2:1)
"After this" (2:12)
"After the two days" (4:43)
"On the morrow" (6:22)
"Two days" (11:6)
"Four days" (11:17)
"Six days" (12:1)
"On the morrow" (12:12)
"After eight days" (20:26)
"After these things," and "afterward" (2:12; 5:14; 11:7, 11; 21:28, 38)

John's Gospel gives us an excellent chronology of Jesus' life. From the synoptic narratives the ministry of Jesus would appear to have lasted for one year only, but from John's narrative it covers a duration of more than three years.

John recorded the visits of Jesus to Jerusalem for the national feasts. The following are his references:

First Feast of Passover (2:12, 13)
"A Feast," almost certainly of Purim (5:1)
Second Feast of Passover (6:4) to which Jesus did not go
Feast of Tabernacles (7:2)
Feast of Dedication (10:22)
Third Feast of Passover (12:1)

It is interesting to note that seven very significant events in the life of Christ are omitted from John's Gospel. The birth of Christ is referred to but not described. The baptism of Christ is implied but not described. There is no record of the temptation of Christ. The transfiguration is not recorded. There is the record of the meaning of the Lord's Supper but not its institution. There is no specific reference to the agony in the garden. John, like Mark and Matthew, omit the ascension of Christ.

The word "Jew" is found once in Matthew, twice in Mark, twice in Luke, and over sixty times in John. The nouns "faith" and "belief" do not occur in John.

None of the Evangelists had as limited a vocabulary as John, but none made better use of what he had. He used fewer words than any of the writers of the Synoptics.

W. Graham Scroggie in his work *Guide to the Gospels* reminds the reader that:

Matthew ends with the resurrection
Mark ends with the ascension
Luke ends with the promise of the Holy Spirit
John ends with the promise of the second coming
Matthew ends with the words, "With me."

Mark ends with the words, "Go ye."
Luke ends with the words, "Tarry ye."
John ends with the word, "Follow."
Matthew ends with special emphasis on the Lord's presence *(28:19, 20)*
Mark ends with special emphasis on the Lord's power *(16:19, 20)*
Luke ends with special emphasis on the Lord's promise *(24:49)*
John ends with special emphasis on the Lord's program *(21:22)*
Each of the four Gospels makes its unique contribution to the recorded life of Christ:

The Promised One is here; see His credentials—*in Matthew*
This is how He worked; see His power—*in Mark*
This is what He was like; see His nature—*in Luke*
This is who He really was; see His Godhead—*in John*

SPECIAL VERSES FOR BIBLE MARKING

1:12	*11:35*	*16:32, 33*
3:14	*12:12, 13*	*17:14*
3:16	*12:32*	*17:24*
5:24	*13:34*	*18:8*
6:20	*14:1*	*18:11*
6:37	*14:6*	*18:37*
6:44	*14:14*	*19:6*
6:47	*14:19*	*19:17-19*
8:6-8	*15:4*	*19:24*
8:32	*15:16*	*19:26-28*
9:25	*16:7*	*20:15, 16-27*
10:27, 28	*16:13*	*21:6*

SPECIAL VERSES TO COMMIT TO MEMORY

1:1	*5:39*	*11:25, 26*
1:12	*6:35*	*12:32*
3:3	*7:37, 38*	*14:1-3*
3:16	*9:25*	*14:6*
4:23	*10:11*	*14:27*
		20:30, 31

GOSPEL OF JOHN FINAL EXAM
Answers on pages 184-187

1. Only Paul wrote more books in the New Testament than John. T____ F____
2. John has more words which are peculiar to his Gospel than Luke has which are peculiar to his Gospel. T____ F____

3. Six characteristic words of the Gospel of John are found in the prologue. They are life, _____ , _____ , witness, _____ and world.

4. The word "parable" occurs once in the King James Version of John's Gospel.   T___ F___

5. The word "proverb" occurs twice in the King James Version of John's Gospel.   F___ F___

6. The three major geographical areas in the Gospel of John are:
_____   _____   _____

7. There are no parables in the Gospel of John.   T___ F___

8. John, the author of the fourth Gospel, was the only disciple not martyred.   T___ F___

9. To whom do these verses refer?
   1:40, 6:8, 9 & 12:20, 22   _____
   3:1-15, 7:50-52 & 19:39   _____
   1:43-46, 6:5-7 & 14:8-11   _____
   11:16, 14:5, 6 & 20:24-29   _____

10. There are 34 individuals referred to in the Gospel of John. _____ of these individuals are named and _____ are unnamed.

11. The Sea of Tiberius, Sea of Galilee & Lake Gennesaret are all the same body of water.   T___ F___

12. Mary Magdalene was the first herald of the risen Christ.   T___ F___

13. Thaddeus or Lebbaeus are other names for _____.

14. Give the titles and authors of two good study books for the Gospel of John.
    _____ by _____
    _____ by _____

15. Quote John 20:30, 31
    _____
    _____
    _____
    _____

16. Repeated Words. (Put the correct letter on the line)
    Verily   ___   (a) 2 times in John
    Believe   ___   (b) 13 times in John
    Father   ___   (c) 390 times in the NT
    World   ___   (d) 9 times in John
    Eternal Life   ___   (e) 4 times in John
    Pneuma   ___   (f) 78 times in John
    Free   ___   (g) 100 times in John
    Logos   ___   (h) 50 times in John
    Sleep   ___   (i) 56 times in John
    Born Again   ___   (j) 18 times in the NT
    Holy Spirit   ___   (k) 2 times in John
    Know   ___   (l) 118 times in John
                               (m) 4 times in the NT

17. Chapter Location: (Put the number of the chapter on the line which best locates the item)
    The betrayal and arrest   _____
    The chapter of unbelief and division   _____
    "Feed" and "Tend"   _____
    Four ways to Christ   _____
    A great sorrow, Savior, and satisfaction   _____

Three aspects of the work of the Holy Spirit _____
Christ prays for Himself _____
The request, test, and reward of faith _____
A midnight interview _____
Jesus gives light, liberty, and life _____

The Triumphal Entry _____
Feast of Tabernacles _____
Fruit, More Fruit, Much Fruit _____
There are seven prayer requests _____
The revelation, rejection, and reception of the Word _____

Discourse on the Bread of Life _____
The New Testament 23rd Psalm _____
The great word here is "Witness" _____
A sevenfold sequence of statement & reply _____
The supper at Bethany _____

The Feast of Dedication _____
The finished work _____
The three denials of Peter _____
The beatitude of service _____
The last and greatest public miracle of Jesus _____

Cleansing the temple _____
His majesty and His meekness _____
The epilogue _____
The Holy of Holies _____
"Eternal Life" is the theme _____

The legacy of peace _____
A total of seven questions with the crucial one
in verse 25 _____
David Brainerd's verse _____
The peak point of popular favor _____
The secret of an untroubled heart _____

Our relation to Christ, Christians, and the world _____
The two appearances of Jesus to His disciples _____
"The hour is come" is the key _____
"What is truth?" _____
Contrasts between Jesus and the Pharisees _____

You may cross out as many as three of the forty questions listed and answer
the following as substitutes
"His own" is the key phrase _____
Curious neighbors, prejudiced Pharisees, cowardly
parents, and bullying Pharisees _____
Recessional and processional _____

18. What is the common thrust or emphasis of these verses?
    2:13; 6:4; 11:55 _____
    4:36, 10:28; 5:39; 17:2 _____

1:29; 1:36; Acts 8:32; 1 Peter 1:19 _____

1:32; 11:33; 13:21; 7:39 _____

1:40; Matthew 4:21, 22; Luke 6:13, 14 _____

19. Give the meaning, translation or identification of the following:
following:

Didymus _____

Thomas _____

Nathanael _____

Cephas _____

Disciples _____

Only begotten _____

Hosanna _____

Bethesda _____

Sign _____

Mansions _____

Band _____

Paraclete _____

Rabbi _____

Siloam _____

Kidron _____

20. Identify the content of the following verses:

1:12: _____

6:35: _____

5:39: _____

15:1 : _____

8:12: _____

12:32: _____

10:7 : _____

14:27: _____

11:25: _____

10:11: _____

14:6 : _____

21. The Old Testament and the Gospel of John (Put the appropriate letter after each passage).

Numbers 21:6-9	_____	(a) John 15
Exodus 12	_____	(b) John 1:9
Psalm 69	_____	(c) John 3:14
		(d) John 2:17
Isaiah 40:3	_____	(e) John 8
Malachi 3:1	_____	(f) John 12:15
Zechariah 9:9	_____	(g) John 2:23
		(h) John 1:23
Psalm 80	_____	(i) John 1:14
Numbers 15:32-36	_____	(j) John 1:6
Isaiah 49:6	_____	
Isaiah 40:5	_____	

22. Distinguish between Golgotha and Calvary.

_____

_____

23. What connection does the cross have with each of the following?

John 19:18 _____
John 19:19-22 _____
John 19:26-27 _____
John 19:28 _____
John 19:30 _____

24. Outline the Analytical Method of Bible Study as set forth in this class.
_____
_____
_____
_____
_____

25. There is no reference to the Destruction of Jerusalem in the Gospel of John.   T___ F___

26. Six of the miracles in the Gospel of John are peculiar to that book.
_____ _____ _____
_____ _____ _____

27. The seven Feasts of Jehovah can be found in one chapter of the Old Testament. This is chapter _____ in the Book of _____.

28. A band of men represented about 1/10th of a legion or about _____ men.

29. Only one of the twelve disciples was not a Galilean.   T___ F___

30. The Jewish day began at _____ and ended at _____.

31. The common thrust of 6:70, 71; 12:1-8; 13:26-30 and 18:2-6 is _____.

32. Quote the following verses:
4:23
_____
_____
_____
_____

6:35
_____
_____
_____
_____

9:25
_____
_____
_____
_____

12:32
_____
_____
_____
_____

14:27
_____
_____
_____
_____

33. Fill in the column for the Gospel of John.

Item	Matthew	Mark	Luke	John
Date	65	59	61	
Chapters	28	16	24	
Verses	1,071	666	1,151	
Period Covered	36 years	4 years	37 years	
Directed to	Jews	Romans	Greeks	
Christ	King	Servant	Man	
Emphasis	Sovereignty	Humility	Humanity	
Sign	Lion	Ox	Man	
Ending	Resurrection	Empty tomb	Promise of the Spirit	
Place of Writing	Antioch	Rome	Rome	
Time to Read	2 hours	1¼ hours	2¼ hours	
Key Verse	27:37	10:45	19:10	
Key Word	Kingdom	Service	Salvation	

34. The author of the Gospel of John was one of two sons of
_____

35. The high point of "belief" was reached in chapter _____.

36. Christ is mentioned in sixteen of the first eighteen verses of chapter _____.

37. Some feel that a portion of chapter _____ might be better located after Luke 21:38.

38. The fact that there is no reference to the _____
_____ which took place in A.D.
_____ has a bearing on the date which one would set for the Gospel of John.

39. There are _____ miracles recorded by the Evangelists.

40. There are _____ interviews which Jesus had with one person and there are _____ interviews which He had with groups of people.

41. The word "_____" is found once in Matthew, twice in Mark, twice in Luke, and over sixty times in John.

42. The nouns "faith" and "belief" do not occur in the Gospel of John.
T____ F____

43. The Gospel of John ends with the _____ and the Gospel of Matthew ends with the resurrection.
44. Nearly one-half of the verses in the Gospel of John contain words of our Lord.   T___ F___
45. Chapter 6 of the Gospel of John contains more verses having the words of Jesus than chapter 2.   T___ F___
46. The 14 discourses in the Gospel of John might be divided into two groups. The first group deals with _____ instruction and are found in chapters _____ through _____ . The second group deals with _____ instruction and are found in chapters _____ through _____.
47. Seven times reference is made to Scripture _____.
48. Over _____ percent of the material in the Gospel of John is peculiar to it.
49. The Feast of _____ is not mentioned elsewhere in the New Testament. It is the modern Jewish Feast of Lights.
50. The "Man of Kerioth" better known as _____ _____ was the only disciple who was not a Galilean.
51. John 13:27 is the only place where _____ is mentioned in the Gospel of John.
52. In John 16:7-15, the Holy Spirit is the One who convicts, _____ and _____ Christ.

Answers to Final Exam

1. True
2. False
3. light; darkness; believe
4. True
5. True
6. Galilee; Samaria; Jerusalem-Judea
7. True
8. True
9. Andrew; Nicodemus; Philip; Thomas
10. 23; 11
11. True
12. True
13. Judas
14. *John, the Gospel of Faith* by Everett Harrison
    John, the Gospel of Belief by Merrill Tenney
15. Many other signs therefore Jesus also performed in the presence of the disciples, which are not written in this book; but these have been written that you may believe that Jesus is the Christ, the Son of God; and that believing you may have life in His name. (NASB)
16. H
    G
    L
    F
    D
    C
    A or K
    E
    J
    A or K
    B
    I
17. 18
    7
    21
    1
    4

    16
    17
    4
    3
    8

    12
    7
    15
    17
    1

    6
    10

1, 5
8
12

10
19
18
13
11

2
18
21
14
17

14
8
7
6
14

15
20
12
18
8

substitutions
13
9
3

18. Passover
    Eternal Life
    Lamb of God
    Holy Spirit
    John
19. Thomas
    Twin
    God has given
    Rock
    Learners
    One of a kind
    Save now
    House of Mercy
    Miracle
    Abiding places
    600 men 1/10 of a legion
    Comforter
    Teacher
    Sent
    Of the Cedars—Dark Waters

20. But as many as received Him, to them gave He the
power . . .
I am the bread of life . . . come . . . never hunger . . . believe . . . never
thirst
Search the Scriptures . . . eternal life . . . they testify of me
I am the true vine . . . Father is the husbandman
I am the light of the world . . . follow Me . . . not walk in darkness
If I be lifted up from the earth, I will draw all men unto Me
I am the door of the sheep
Peace I leave . . . give . . . not as world giveth . . . let not heart be
troubled
I am the resurrection and the life . . . believeth . . . though dead, will live
I am the good Shepherd . . . giveth His life for the sheep
I am the way, the truth, the life . . . come by Me

21. C
G
D
H
J
F
A
E
B
I

22. Golgotha-Hebrew; Calvary-Latin

23. Three Crosses
Transcription
Third word—"Woman behold . . ."
Fifth word—"I thirst"
Sixth word—"It is finished"

24. Who?
What?
When?
Where?
Why?
Wherefore?

25. True

26. Water to wine; Healing of invalid; Lazarus; Healing of off. son; Healing of
blind from birth; Siloam; Net full of fish

27. 23; Leviticus

28. 600

29. True

30. sunset; sunset

31. Judas

32. Yet time is coming and has now come when the true worshipers will
worship the Father in spirit and truth, for they are the kind of worshipers
the Father seeks.

I am the bread of life. He who comes to me will never grow hungry, and
he who believes in me will never be thirsty.

Whether He is a sinner or not, I don't know. I do know one thing, I was
blind but now I see.

But I, when I am lifted up from the earth will draw all men to Myself.

Peace I leave with you, my peace I give you. I do not give to you as the world gives. Do not let your hearts be troubled and do not be afraid.

33. 90
    21
    879
    4 years
    World
    Son of God
    Deity
    Eagle
    Promise of the 2nd Coming
    Ephesus
    1½ hours
    20:30, 31
    Believe
34. Zebedee
35. 12
36. 1
37. 8
38. destruction of Jerusalem; 70
39. 35
40. 14; 20
41. Jew
42. True
43. Second Coming
44. True
45. True
46. public; 1; 12; private; 12; 16
47. being fulfilled
48. 90 percent
49. Dedication
50. Judas Iscariot
51. Satan
52. guides; glorifies

BIBLIOGRAPHY

Barclay, William. *The Gospel of John*. 2 vols. Philadelphia: The Westminster Press, 1975.

Barnes, Albert. *Notes on the New Testament* (Volume on Luke and John). Grand Rapids: Baker Book House, 1960.

Barrett, C. K. *The Gospel according to St. John: An Introduction with Commentary and Notes on the Greek Text.* Second Edition. Philadelphia: The Westminster Press, 1978.

Baxter, J. Sidlow. *Explore the Book,* vol. 5. London: Marshall, Morgan and Scott, 1955.

Boice, James Montgomery. *Witness and Revelation in the Gospel of John.* Grand Rapids: Zondervan Publishing House, 1970.

Brown, R. E. *The Gospel According to John: Introduction, Translation, and Notes.* The Anchor Bible, vols. 29 and 29A. Garden City: Doubleday, 1966, 1970.

Calvin, John. *Commentary on the Gospels.* Grand Rapids: Associated Publishers and Authors, n.d.

Exell, Joseph S. *The Biblical Illustrator,* vols. 1, 2, 3. New York: Fleming H. Revell, n.d.

Garrison, Webb B. *Sermon Seeds from the Gospels.* Westwood, N.J.: Fleming H. Revell Co., 1958.

Gundry, Robert H. *A Survey of the New Testament.* Grand Rapids: Zondervan Publishing House, 1970.

Guthrie, Donald. *New Testament Introduction.* Downer's Grove, Illinois: Inter-Varsity Press, 1973.

Harrison, Everett F. *John: The Gospel of Faith.* Chicago: Moody Press, 1962.

Harrison, Norman B. *His Gospel of Life, Love and Light.* Chicago: Moody Press, 1929.

Hastings, James (Ed.). *The Great Texts of the Bible, James and Jude.* Edinburgh: T. & T. Clark, 1912.

Hendriksen, William. *Bible Survey.* Grand Rapids: Baker Book House, 1949.

Hovey, Alvah. *Commentary on John*. Philadelphia: American Baptist Publication Society, 1885.

Hudson, Roland V. *Bible Survey Outlines*. Grand Rapids: Wm. B. Eerdmans Publishing Company, 1954.

Jensen, Irving L. *John*. Chicago: Moody Press, 1970.

Lange, Johann P. *Commentary on the Holy Scriptures*, vol. 9. New York: Charles Scribner & Co., 1868.

Laurin, Roy L. *John: Life Eternal*. Chicago: Moody Press, 1972.

Lee, Robert. *The Outlined John*. London: Pickering & Inglis, n.d.

Macaulay, J. C. *Obedient Unto Death*. Grand Rapids: Wm. B. Eerdmans Publishing Co., 1942.

Meyer, F. B. *Gospel of John: The Life and Light of Man*. Fort Washington: Christian Literature Crusade, 1970.

Morgan, G. Campbell. *The Gospel According to John*. New York: Fleming H. Revell Co., n.d.

Morgan, G. C. *Living Messages of the Books of the Bible*. New York: Fleming H. Revell Co., 1912.

Morris, L. *Commentary on the Gospel of John* (NIC). Grand Rapids: Wm. B. Eerdmans, 1971.

Murray, Andrew. *The True Vine*. Chicago: Moody Press, n.d.

Nicoll, W. Robertson. *The Expositor's Bible*. New York: A. C. Armstrong & Son, 1903.

Pentz, Croft M. *Expository Outlines on the Gospel of John*. Grand Rapids: Baker Book House, 1974.

Perry, Lloyd M. and Culver, Robert. *How to Search the Scriptures*. Grand Rapids: Baker Book House, 1967.

Rainsford, Marcus. *Our Lord Prays for His Own*. Chicago: Moody Press, 1955.

Reynolds, H. R. and Croskery, T. *Pulpit Commentary: The Gospel of John*. Grand Rapids: Wm. B. Eerdmans Publishing Co., 1950.

Richardson, Alan. *The Gospel According to Saint John*. New York: Collier Books, 1959.

Richardson, Alan. *The Miracle Stories of the Gospels*. London: S C M Press, 1941.

Robertson, Archibald Thomas. *Word Pictures in the New Testament*. Vol. V. New York: Harper & Brothers, 1932.

Scroggie, W. Graham. *A Guide to the Gospels*. London: Pickering & Inglis, 1948.

Scroggie, W. Graham. *Know Your Bible*. vol. 11. London: Pickering & Inglis, 1940.

Speer, Robert E. *John's Gospel: The Greatest Book in the World*. New York: Fleming H. Revell Co., 1915.

Stevenson, Dwight E. *Preaching on the Books of the New Testament*. New York: Harper & Brothers Publishers, 1956.

Tenney, Merrill C. *John: The Gospel of Belief*. Grand Rapids: Wm. B. Eerdmans Publishing Co., 1948.

Tenney, Merrill C. *New Testament Survey*. Grand Rapids: Wm. B. Eerdmans Publishing Co., 1961.

Thomas, W. H. Griffith. *The Apostle John: Studies in His Life and Writings*. Grand Rapids: Wm. B. Eerdmans Publishing Co., 1946.

Trench, Richard Chenevix. *Studies in the Gospels*. London: Macmillan & Co., 1867.

Vincent, M. R. *Word Studies in the New Testament*. McLean, Virginia: MacDonald Publishing Co., 1888.